The

Fabulous Reinvention

of

Sunday School

the Fabulous Reinvention of Sunday School

Transformational Techniques for Reaching and Teaching Kids

AARON REYNOLDS

ZONDERVAN®

WILLOW
Willow Creek Resources

ZONDERVAN.com/
AUTHORTRACKER
follow your favorite authors

We want to hear from you. Please send your comments about this book to us in care of zreview@zondervan.com. Thank you.

ZONDERVAN®

The Fabulous Reinvention of Sunday School
Copyright © 2007 by Willow Creek Association

Requests for information should be addressed to:

Zondervan, *Grand Rapids, Michigan 49530*

Library of Congress Cataloging-in-Publication Data

Reynolds, Aaron, 1970 –
        The fabulous reinvention of Sunday school : transformational techniques for reaching and teaching kids / Aaron Reynolds.
            p. cm.
        ISBN-13: 978-0-310-27433-9
        ISBN-10: 0-310-27433-8
        1. Christian education of children. I. Title.
    BV1475.3.R49 2007
    268'.432 – dc22   2006102158

Interior design by Mark Sheeres

Illustrations by David Barneda

Printed in the United States of America

16 • 20 19 18 17 16 15 14 13 12

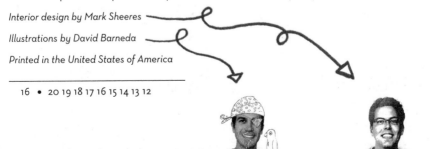

GIRAFFES WEAR
SUNGLASSES BECAUSE
THEY ARE SO CLOSE
TO THE SUN

CONTENTS

TO

DEANNA ARMENTROUT

for being a squeaky-wheeled voice in the wilderness,
for drawing me into children's ministry with her excellence, vision, and passion,
and for pushing me to ever new heights along the way.

AND

To **Christine Anderson**

a Jedi of an editor and a friend...
without her deft guidance, this book would be a jumble of scattered and incoherent thoughts.
I mean, more than it is now.

ACKNOWLEDGMENTS

I need to send a serious thank you out to several people whose keen input was crucial to the development of this book.

✶ Thanks to Denise Dyer and Lynn Hansen, who were both wonderful sounding boards as I wrote, ruthlessly poking holes in my thinking, my humor, and my sentence structure ... curse them.

✶ Thanks to Debbie Nichols, Jim Marshall, Tom Nagy, and Scott Reisdorf, for their insightful stories from the front lines of children's ministry, and to the scads of other children's ministry champs who graciously shared the stories that never made it all the way to the pages of this book.

✶ Thanks to David Barneda, who illustrated this book, and Mark Sheeres, who designed it. These guys were a blast to work with, and it's because of their brilliance that this book looks so weird and funky.

✶ Thanks to my wife, Michelle, and my kids, Ethan and Reese, who endured my writing mania with so much grace.

✶ Finally, thanks to the world-class creative team in Promiseland that I had the fortune to work with in the weekend trenches for so many years ... Arnez, Kevin, Deanna, Marta, Kathy, Holly, Hyoo-bear, Holly D., Kerri, Bob, Dugan, Christy ... and loads others. You pushed me, challenged me, sharpened me, and ... at times ... irritated me. Thank you.

AND THANKS TO HAROLD, THE ACKNOWLEDGMENTS—READING PENGUIN!

INTRODUCTION:

TEACHING REINVENTED!

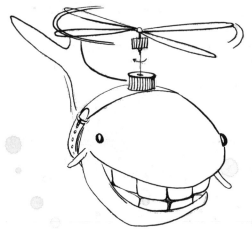

Imagine it.

You are walking by the teaching room on Sunday morning and are alarmed by the uproarious laughter of kids coming from within. Certain that the children must have mutinied at last and taken over the room in a violent revolt, you cautiously open the door. You're stunned at what you see. The laughter comes, not from the kids' pleasure at slowly lowering one of your fellow teachers into a tank full of piranhas but, instead, from their joy at hearing the story of Joshua and Caleb told in a hilarious and highly interactive way. As the lesson ends, the kids charge out into the real world, jazzed about what they've heard, skilled up to do life differently when Monday rolls around.

Pretty sweet scenario, huh?

This is what we long for. Kids who are transfixed and transformed by the Bible. We all catch glimpses of it from time to time, but what if it was the norm? What if every weekend you were able to experience the thrill of delivering *transformational teaching*?

Regardless of the size, budget, space limitations, or style of your children's ministry, transformational teaching is well within reach. But it requires us to rethink some things. It requires a little reinvention of Sunday school.

Too often our Sunday school teaching focuses on transferring "head knowledge" from teacher to student. It's a method most kids already experience five days a week in school. But the Bible isn't multiplication tables or a list of countries and capitals. If we deliver only "head knowledge," we've stopped at the halfway point.

Imagine an approach that ignites kids' imaginations, that elicits awe, that leaves them breathless about God's power, that leaves them truly changed. Imagine teaching kids the Bible in a way that leads to true transformation.

Transformational teaching...

> ... makes a powerful emotional connection to kids, impacting them with the wonderment of the Bible.
>
> ... brings the Bible to *life* by using creativity in powerful and compelling ways.
>
> ... involves kids experientially in the learning so the Bible becomes unforgettable.
>
> ... jam-packs every lesson with application that equips kids to live God-centered lives in the real world.

With some techniques and tools for reaching and teaching kids, you can make your lessons truly transformational.

If you're a ministry leader, I hope you'll read along for the ride, but this book is designed, first and foremost, for teachers—Sunday school teachers, large group communicators, upfront presenters, whatever you call yourself. If you teach the kids on Sunday (we're talking elementary-aged kids and younger), this book has your name written all over it. This isn't a book about activities, coloring pages or conversation starters to supplement your teaching; it's a book about you. It's about how to take your ability to creatively teach kids to soaring new heights. While some chapters cast vision—challenging your thinking and motivating you to take up new practices—most are stuffed to the seams with practical techniques to help you bring power to your teaching, whether you teach six kids every Sunday ... or 206.

So imagine it ...

A children's ministry in which transformational teaching is the order of the day.

> Where the walls rattle every weekend with Holy Spirit power.

> Where prepared teachers teach powerful lessons that leave kids dumbstruck with awe about God's might and presence in their lives.

> Where creative methods excite kids about the Bible to the point that they live life differently on Monday as a result of Sunday.

Imagine yourself not imagining anymore.
Sounds fabulous to me.

I BELIEVE I CAN FLY...

ding ding

PART ONE

Creating
an
Atmosphere
of
Excellence

Excellence attracts people. People leave jobs and move to new ones over excellence. Excellence dictates people's choices about TV shows, vacation spots, and even cell phone providers. No doubt about it, people are drawn to excellence.

Excellence inspires kids. If you think kids are an easy audience, think again. There's a reason that those fifth-grade boys sit in the back with their arms crossed and an *impress me* look on their faces. Because kids aren't easily impressed. But they respond to true excellence.

Excellence honors God. God had some pretty strong words in Malachi 1:6–8 for some of his followers who showed up at the altar thinking *good enough is good enough*. God wants our very best.

In children's ministry, we would probably all agree that we want excellence. But too often we mistakenly get the idea that excellence requires lots of money and tons of special effects.

Not true.

In fact, if you asked me to name the key practices a ministry can embrace to create a teaching atmosphere that screams excellence, I'd give you my top four: memorization, rehearsal, evaluation, and a strategic teaching rotation.

Then I'd point out that they don't cost a dime. Just a mindset shift.

So I know you didn't ask. But here they are anyway.

CHAPTER 1

COMMITTED TO MEMORY

12welve years ago, like a rookie stepping up to bat for the first time, I timidly took my place in front of a roomful of second and third graders and taught my first Bible lesson in children's ministry. A seasoned actor, I was nevertheless fairly freaked out by the fiercely intimidating audience gawking at me in such close proximity, hanging on (and surely evaluating) my every word, and waiting to hit the gong or grab the hook should I fail to earn 25 minutes of their attention. I didn't hit a homerun that weekend, but I survived, and perhaps more importantly, so did they.

Thinking back, I can now evaluate my first lesson with a clearer lens. The lesson was shaky (or maybe it was my hands that were doing the shaking) due in large part to my deathly fear of the seven-year-olds I faced. The lesson was probably a bit boring, though I justified using at least three completely unrelated videos, eating up about four minutes apiece, and giving me a few moments of precious relief. The lesson was probably slight enough on solid Bible content to make a deacon whimper. But among all the "opportunities for growth" my first lesson contained, I can affirm one thing I did right. The lesson was memorized. All 12 pages of it.

Over 400 Bible lessons later, I regularly stand before scads of kids with the confidence of a seasoned lion tamer. I put tremendous effort into injecting every lesson with an infusion of variety and creativity. And I make sure all that creativity serves one purpose: to elevate clear and solid Bible teaching. Many things have changed about

WARNING
7-YEAR-OLD PIRANHAS

my approach to teaching the Bible since my tenderfooted beginnings. But one thing remains tried, true, and unchanged. I still memorize my lessons. Every word.

WHY MEMORIZE?

If you asked me to name one thing that has the power to take the teaching in your ministry to the next level (we're talking purely practical things here, putting aside prayer and the presence of the Holy Spirit and that awesome stuff for just a sec), I would say "memorization" every time. When it comes to creating excellent and powerful Bible teaching, I am committed to memorization.

I know.

Memorization? It takes time.

True.

I want to be free to be my natural spontaneous self.

I hear you.

I want to be released to move with the Holy Spirit.

Who wouldn't?

I'M NO GOOD AT MEMORIZING.

I'm feelin' for ya.

So why? Why should I memorize?

Fair question. Here are the facts of the matter. Despite all those incredibly valid concerns, memorization brings intentionality, Holy Spirit connection, growth, and power to teaching kids like nothing else I know. Interested? Then keep reading.

scary but true!

Create Intentionality

I once watched a weekend teacher deliver a lesson that began with the story of Cain and Abel and ended by explaining that the reason we celebrate Easter with Easter eggs is because the stone in front of Jesus' tomb was egg-shaped.

True story.

This teacher's ministry leader had instructed him to "just get the gist of it" and to "hit the main points." As I hung on for dear life during the meandering message, trying desperately to glean a single clear nugget of truth to walk away with, it was clear that this lesson lacked something critical: Intentionality.

Has anyone (a leader perhaps, not mentioning any names, of course) ever handed you a teaching script and basically said "just hit the main points"? That's a major disservice—to you *and* the kids. Words spoken from the front of your teaching room on Sunday can change the choices kids will make that week—not to mention their eternities—so every word counts. And don't forget that the Bible warns not many of us to be teachers, because we will be held accountable for what we teach. Yikes! This is serious business. Leaders who oversee children's ministries need to know the words that are spoken during lessons each weekend. And, as a teacher, I want some support and accountability backing me up as I lay it on the line and teach God's Word. A set teaching script gets everyone on the same page, and the value of memorization ensures that the teaching script is honored.

NOT TO WORRY, I'LL HIT ALL THE MAIN POINTS

SCRIPT ↓

TO BE OR NOT TO BE, THAT'S THE THINGY ... UH WHAT COMES NEXT?

Tune In to the Holy Spirit

I recently heard a teaching volunteer give the excuse I most commonly hear for not embracing memorization: "I want to be free for the Holy Spirit to move." That's an honorable desire. But here's another perspective worth giving some think-time to: the Holy Spirit honors a prepared teacher. The Holy Spirit meets me consistently in my memorization time, equipping me to teach from a strong and prepared place.

Let's get real for a second. When I'm in the middle of teaching an unprepared lesson, I'm usually not tuning into the Holy Spirit. I can't. I'm too busy trying to remember what comes next or figuring out why I'm talking about Easter eggs instead of Cain and Abel and how I can get back to the subject at hand. On the flip side, when I'm memorized, I am free! I'm not worrying about what comes next, because I know what comes next. It is then, and only then, that I am truly aware enough during a lesson to get good signal reception from above. I sense that small voice that says: "The kids didn't quite get what you just said about forgiving an enemy (it's a tricky concept anyway, right?), so just unpack it with another sentence or two." Or the Holy Spirit tunes me into my audience enough to know that those three fourth-grade boys in the back are burping the alphabet instead of listening (don't pretend they don't), so I need to just soften my voice enough to draw them back in … and then move on. These are messages I would miss if I were all wrapped up in my head searching for the right words.

The truth of the matter is this … the Holy Spirit is going to show up and do his work anyway. The question that remains is: Will he work *in spite of* me or will he partner *with* me?

HOLY SPIRIT RADIO
fifty trillion megawatts of pure power!

Risk Growth

Still struggling with this whole memorization thing? Feeling that your leaders would be crossing the line to make such a brazen and outlandish request? Go back to the excellence thing. Do you want excellence? Most of us would say yes. But then we have to take that next dangerous step and ask: Am I willing to do what is needed to make ball-out-of-the-park teaching possible?

CRUMPLED NOTES

Memorization makes excellence possible. Once you overcome the hurdle of memorization, you'll discover a whole new set of skills and abilities you never knew existed. You will be freed up to make amazing and creative moments happen in your lessons that could never happen if you still had one eye glued to the outline sticking out of your pocket.

DON'T NEED 'EM NO MORE!

If your ministry has pushed past this hurdle and affirms the value of memorization, your leaders have given you a gift. They have challenged and equipped you with one of the major tools you will need to take your teaching to the next level. Nuances of timing and pacing and moment-making—things that were never within grasp before—are now possible. And while you may feel the growing pains of such a change (and be tempted to bail out over the issue), you will find the excellence of your ministry, and your own personal gifts, increasing. When that happens, everyone wins. You get to experience the blessing and excitement of your gifts taking off into orbit. Your ministry and leaders win because your excellence draws even more volunteers to the ministry. And the kids win because they experience the impact of your ever-increasingly dynamic teaching ... and are transformed by it.

MORE CRUMPLED NOTES!!

CRUMPLE
CRUMPLE
CRUMPLE

Play for Power

Along with intentionality, Holy Spirit impact, and mighty personal growth, memorization brings power to teaching. Power comes when kids experience a teacher proclaiming truths rather than reading them off a cheat sheet. Authority comes when a gifted storyteller breathes real life into the story of Jesus healing the paralytic rather than just reporting the facts like an anchor on the five o'clock news.

Not only do kids sense the power and authority in a lesson that has been properly committed to memory, but you grow in confidence and ownership of your role in the ministry. You begin to sense the importance of the role you play—that your job is not just to get through the lesson each week (we've all felt that, huh?) but to proclaim the Bible with creativity, to bring stories to life before the kids' eyes, to create unforgettable moments that shape and transform young lives.

Not convinced? Don't take my word for it; take it from Debbie Nichols, a weekend teacher at Grace Community Church in Columbia, Maryland. Debbie was a staunch anti-memorization rebel who became a die-hard convert. "I firmly believed that if everything was memorized I would sound like a bit of a robot," Debbie told me recently. "So I looked over my lessons a few times to get the "gist" of it. I also thought the Holy Spirit would kind of 'give' me the words I needed to say in the moment. Because I tend to be wordy, I could easily get off on tangents and would lose my train of thought. It made me feel very nervous every time I went to teach."

The change came when Debbie's leader, Denise, lobbed a big old hand-grenade of a challenge into her lap by asking Debbie to memorize her lessons. Gritting her teeth, Debbie nevertheless took on the challenge and, within a few short weeks, had a completely different perspective.

"Memorization transformed my teaching!" Debbie now boasts. "I still get nervous, but God shows up. Each week I commit the lesson to prayer and ask God to guide me in my teaching, but I have to do my part and have the lesson memorized for God to really work. I have so much more power and authority in my teaching. I can

YAAAA HOOOOoo...

OOPS! GOT A LITTLE CARRIED AWAY CRUMPLING THINGS...

concentrate on the kids and emotionally connect with them. Because the words are memorized, they flow freely—I never have to stop to find my place. Just this past week I was teaching a lesson on John the Baptist—the power in the room was so real. It was a God moment, and once again affirmed my new belief that there is freedom in having things memorized."

Before being committed to memorization, Debbie characterized her experience of teaching with phrases like, "get through it," "hit the main points," "fly by the seat of my pants."

But nowadays, her teaching conjures up a new vocabulary.

P O W E R

AUTHORITY

TRANSFORMATION

F R E E D O M .

Not a bad way to spend a weekend.

Please see page 26 for a note regarding this illustration.

TRICKS OF THE TRADE

"Okay, I'm convinced," you say. "At least, more than I was ten minutes ago. But I've never memorized before. How do I do it?"

Good question. I thought you'd never ask.

Compartmentalize It

The first teaching script I ever sat down to memorize was 12 pages long. Daunting? Uh, yeah. The prospect of memorizing all those pages did one doozy of a head-trip on me. But I soon realized something ...

The first three pages of the script contained a simple little game show to set up the point of the day: that Jesus can do anything. Huh! Those three pages all fit together into one cohesive section.

And don't look now, but the next four pages were made up of the story of Jesus healing the paralytic man. Section two, the story. I could remember that.

And check it out! The last couple pages of the script were all made up of specific life illustration examples designed to drive the point home. Section three!

Suddenly, it was all gellin' together. Those gazillion words spread out over 12 vast overwhelming pages actually fit together nice and neat into three cohesive, make-sense sections. Compartments. And while I felt like I could never scale a mountain like 12 pages, I could maneuver a three-section molehill with a fair amount of ease. And my brain, which has limited compartments itself, rejoiced.

Write on It

I'm a very visual learner, so when I'm wrestling with what comes next, I actually visualize the physical page of my script. I exploit my learning style to the fullest. When I break my script into those tidy little compartments, I actually write directly on the script. I draw a box around each section. I write a fat juicy "1" at the top of section one. I also write section titles or other cues directly onto the script. Stuff like: "The Game Show," "The Paralytic," "Get answers from audience," "Don't forget to pray"—whatever works. That way, when I think back to the page on the script, I also think back to these simple visual cues.

How about colored pens or highlighters? Color code sections to give yourself a visual hook on which to hang your memory. Section one is blue. Section two is orange. Section three? Fuchsia. Fuchsia doesn't get used near enough in my opinion.

Count the number of knives to find out what page you're on! (For the answer, go to page 23.)

Post-Its anyone? A few Post-Its here and there work wonders. Whatever you need to do to give yourself a little visual roadmap as you travel through the lesson. The goal is that by the time you get in front of kids, you aren't thinking about these clues at all anymore. But on the journey from total unmemorized panic to rock-solid memorization, these visual road signs are your friends.

Rewrite It

Some people I know go the extra step and actually rewrite the entire script in longhand. In fact, according to Ron Cronovich, a professor of economics at the University of Nevada, "Studies on learning behavior show that the *process* of recopying your notes helps cement the material into your long-term memory, so you will benefit even if you never look at your recopied notes again." I don't know a whole lot about economics, but I remember David, a former children's ministry colleague of mine, telling me about how he rewrote every lesson into a spiral notebook. To me, this method sounds as painful as having the entire script tattooed onto my hindquarters, and I wouldn't go near it with a ten-foot pen, but some people insist it makes memorization a breeze. Okay, not a breeze. Breezier.

Record It

Ever get a song stuck in your head after a few listens, and you just can't get it out? Sure, we all have. Just between you and me, there are times I'd pay good money to stop a certain overplayed Avril Lavigne tune from rattling around in my cranium. Well, while your teaching script may not be as catchy as an Avril ditty, you can still put the same basic principles to work to help you memorize.

Yay for sticky notes! We're the best!

We're the best thing since...since...um... since the un-sticky kind of note.

Back in my day, the un-sticky kind was all we had.

Know what else works really good?

What?

Re-writing your lessons . . .

. . . and recording them, don't forget!

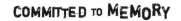

Give this a try: read your teaching script into a tape recorder or CD. You can play it over and over on the way to and from work. Chances are, after several times through, you'll be saying the lesson right along with the tape. Then the only challenging part is to get it out of your head once the weekend has come and gone. Good luck with that.

A cautionary note. Don't get so locked into delivering a lesson just like you did it on the tape that you can't add nuances that come with rehearsal, such as pacing, passion, energy, and silence (the kind of stuff we'll work on in Part 2).

I'm no longer a rookie, but ever since that first valiant teaching effort many years ago, I continually remind myself that the worn carpet of my little teaching room is holy ground. It is on that hallowed threadbare floor that God prepares me to be used by him to change kids lives. The stakes are high. And if showing up with my full game each weekend means putting in the time to memorize my lesson, then I have only one thing to say . . .

Game on.

— A note from the designer —

Dear Reader,

I would like to apologize for the scratched-out illustration on page 22. My idea was to draw a body-building Supreme Court Justice who was a butterfly and who had next Friday off work—thus illustrating the concepts of *power, authority, transformation,* and *freedom,* respectively. But I had a rotten time of it, and it just didn't work out.

Hopefully things work out better with the rest of the illustrations. There's still a long way to go in this book.

If you'd like, you can take a stab at it yourself. Space for drawing has been provided below.

With kindest regards and sincerest regrets,

—The Designer

DRAW HERE

THE PRACTICE OF PRACTICING

OF

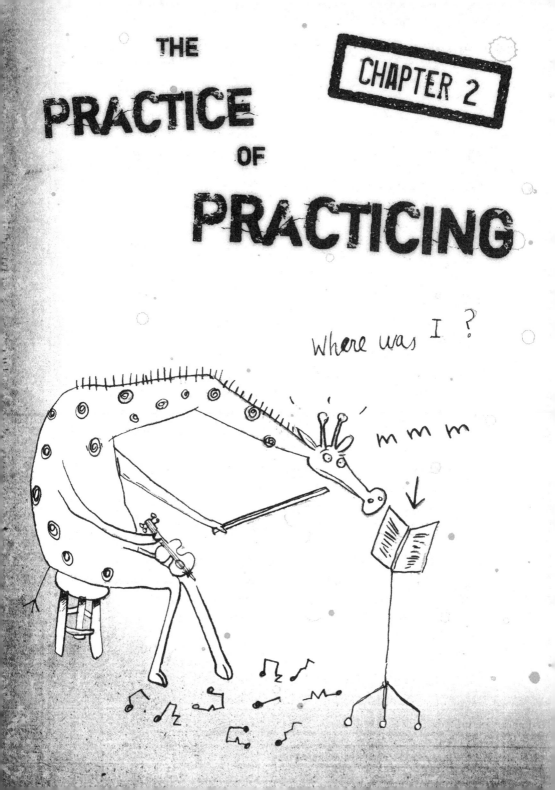

CHAPTER 2

Where was I?

m m m

Congratulations! Your daughter just got the lead in her school's production of *The Wizard of Oz*. To fulfill this "volunteer" role, she will attend after-school rehearsals for two and a half months solid. And I'll bet my ruby slippers that she'll be only too happy about it.

You know the drill. The music teacher will sit the cast down at the first rehearsal and give them the spiel.

"I expect you all to be at every rehearsal," she'll say.

No problem.

"You need to be prepared when you get here and ready to work."

Gotcha.

"On top of that, you need to go home when we're done and get your homework done. No letting your grades slip because of this production."

Roger.

"Now let's get to work!"

Yippee!

Your daughter is only too delighted to hold fast to the music teacher's rehearsal regiment. She's thrilled to be using her talent as part of something excellent. She wants her Dorothy to be the best. She knows rehearsal will get her there.

Is this music teacher a maniacal tyrant?

No way.

Are her standards too high?

Not on your life. She should expect no less from her cast.

But when it comes to the prospect of practice in Sunday school, we tend to do some serious soft-pedaling. Why do we flinch at the thought of putting in practice time on our Bible lesson? Why do we check our expectations of excellence at the Sunday school door? Personally, I'd like to see our bar even higher than the local production of *The Wizard of Oz*. So what do we lack?

The brains? Please.

The heart? Spare me.

The courage? Hmmm ... maybe.

We're not likely to drift into life-changing story-telling, all accidental-like.

We'll rarely stumble into transformational moments that bring the Bible to life with power.

Okay fine, that one time. But that was a fluke—admit it. Mostly, powerful moments have to be rehearsed.

If you've ever taught more than one service on a weekend, you know the thrill of getting to that second service and having things just cook. Everyone knows what they're doing, the delivery is strong, the kids are *so* much more engaged ... right? You feel like, "If only the other service had gone this well!" Why does that second service sizzle?

Because you used the first one as rehearsal!

Rehearsal works. It makes for powerful lessons packed with planned moments. It allows you to use whatever technical elements that you may have at your disposal (stuff like lights, sound, and video) to their fullest. It allows you to make seamless transitions between teaching and other elements like music or puppetry, instead of those awkward "uh ... what comes next?" moments.

Yep. Rehearsal works.

But the real question is ... How do we work rehearsal? How do we courageously embrace the practice of practicing to create lessons that shine like the Emerald City on a sunny day?

Feel like you need a rehearsal handbook?

I'm on it.

Let's get practical about practice.

MIDWEEK REHEARSAL

A single midweek rehearsal is the perfect place for everyone to get their bearings. An hour and a half is ideal. Two hours is great. If you can, set rehearsals at a time when you and others are around the church anyway. Does your church offer a midweek service? Perfect! You could hold your rehearsals before or after the midweek service.

Keep midweek rehearsals consistent. It's a dangerous game to start adjusting rehearsals for everyone's individual schedule. A consistent and standard commitment lets teachers (and actors and puppeteers) know what to expect. Everyone knows from the start if they can sign onto this serving commitment, because the scheduled midweek rehearsal is just part of the serving commitment. I'd rather have someone decline the opportunity from the start because of a scheduling conflict than say "let's make it work" and keep everyone else in a constant state of frustration because that person's PDA is on calendar-overload. Set a schedule and stick to it. It honors everyone's time.

Once you've got a consistent midweek time set, now what? What do you do with your two hours?

WEDNESDAY NIGHT

NEXT WED. NIGHT

NEXT WED. NIGHT

NEXT WED. NIGHT

NEXT WED. NIGHT

Just Do It

I'm often surprised to see rehearsals that consist of everyone just talking about what they think they'll do.

NEXT WED. NIGHT

NEXT WED. NIGHT

NEXT

During midweek rehearsal, don't just sit around and *talk* about the lesson. Get on your feet and *do* it. Practice.

Decide your movement (this is called *blocking*), actually setting detailed movement patterns throughout the lesson. Determine when you will sit on a stool, when you will stand, when you will move out into the audience, when you will sit on the edge of the stage. These details give the lesson flow and rhythm and help bring it to life.

Work through the dynamics of the lesson, sculpting moments along the way. When is the story soft and poignant? When is it fast and driving? When is it casual and interactive? When will you go into the audience and get responses from the kids? Practicing and determining these details at midweek rehearsal gives you a chance to try things out and see what works. By having these specifics of the lesson practiced and resolved before Sunday ever rolls around, you give yourself renewed confidence and your presentation strength.

WEEKEND REHEARSAL

T minus 60 minutes until service starts, and one word describes the mood on Sunday ... chaos! Once the weekend hits, time is limited. Because of this reality, Sunday morning rehearsals are often scattered and frustrating experiences ... a race against the clock just to cram something quasi-useful into this time. Running an efficient and productive rehearsal on the weekend just takes a little planning. It also means a willingness to schedule people early enough to actually get something done.

Here's a weekend rehearsal schedule I've used with great success. Since it assumes three weekend services and use of elements like drama and music, you may need to adapt or simplify it to suit the needs of your ministry. The key is to have a set schedule ... plan the work, and work the plan. The payoff is a calmer, more productive weekend prep time and improved excellence in the long run. And a walloping spoonful of professionalism *(don't cringe at that word)*, which equals vision, vision, vision for whoever happens to be watching ... parents, potential volunteers, or the pastor.

Saturday Rehearsal

12:30 — 2:00

Tech Set Up

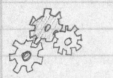

My team often doesn't get the owner-ship of the room until 12:30 (the high school ministry meets there 'til then). Set-up of lights, sound, and the teaching stage happens here, overseen by a volunteer tech team of two to three people.

2:00 — 2:45

Drama Rehearsal

Drama gets the room and the stage, giving the actors 45 minutes to work on the stage with set and props, overseen by a drama director. As the lead teacher (sometimes we call it the "producer") of the entire creative lesson, I stay to observe, to give the director a 5-minute warning, and to give any important feedback.

2:45 — 3:30

Music Rehearsal

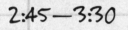

Music leaders and/or any bands get the room and the stage. Forty-five minutes is spent working through the music/worship element in the space.

3:30 — 3:45   Teaching Team Huddle

The team circles up on the floor. As the producer, I cast vision about the weekend lesson to the whole team (teachers, actors, singers, tech team, etc.), and walk through the details of the program so everyone is on the same page. We pray together.

3:45 — 4:30   Run-Through

WHOOOSH!

We do the entire teaching program, incorporating all elements, with tech.

No one stops the run-through except me, the producer. Since this is the tech team's first chance through it, I usually stop only for tech cues. If we stop, we back up and try the section again, smoothing out transitions, and moving on. Time is limited, so I must be efficient. Since I am often both the producer and the teacher, I must keep calm and level, working my own teaching during this run-through but also leading the team effectively. As the producer of the room, I must be well prepared.

4:30   Rehearsal Stops

The room opens for kids for the pre-service games and activities, prior to the 5:00 p.m. service.

Sunday Morning Rehearsal

8:00

Everyone is called for one run-through. We've been through it last night and we de-briefed the lesson (evaluation) after the 5:00 service, so I can expect this time to run smoothly. This is just a once-through to make sure everyone is awake and on their game.

8:30

The room opens in anticipation of the 9:00am service.

Just for giggles, let's imagine an alternate version, one that might be closer to reality for a church with fewer services. Let's say that there is no Saturday night service, just two services on Sunday: a 9:00 a.m. and an 11:00 a.m. Would I call a Saturday afternoon rehearsal? Probably not. I might call the tech crew to set up on Saturday if that was an option. So what would I do? Probably something like this:

Sunday Morning Rehearsal

alternate reality

7:00 — 7:25   Drama Rehearsal

I know it's early, but most teachers and actors agree it's better to come early than to have to show up on both Saturday and

Sunday. I agree. If I could get away with it, I might call people at 6:00 a.m., but I'd probably get flogged by the team for that. No problem. Everything can work with a 7:00 a.m. start if I'm calm and efficient. Everyone must realize that every minute counts, a vision I must cast continually to promote a productive rehearsal ethic. No straggling in late. A productive rehearsal ethic elevates the work we do, and communicates that this is serious business, worthy of our best efforts.

7:25 — 7:50   Music Rehearsal

7:50 — 8:00   Teaching Team Huddle

I don't skip or gloss over this. It is here that I cast vision and instill in the team the sense that they are part of something great this weekend—which they are. We pray and ask God's blessing on our efforts.

8:00 — 8:30   Run-Through

Again, a must-do. See the "Run-through" section below. Typically the room needs to open at 8:30 to accept kids. This may feel tight time-wise, but I may be able to negotiate regularly opening the room at 8:45 instead of 8:30, buying the teaching team 15 more minutes.

8:30

Room opens in anticipation of the 9:00 a.m. service.

THE RUN-THROUGH

I come from a theater background, so the idea of "getting through the whole thing" is just ingrained in me. This is a practice and a value that I have carried over with me into my work in teaching creative children's ministry lessons. Whatever different elements make up my weekend lesson … whether it includes teaching, drama, music, tech, sword swallowers (just joking on that one … *or am I?*) or simply a creative storyteller with a mic … I don't want the first time I actually get through the whole lesson to be at the first service.

What's the DNA of a successful run-through? While every ministry will work things a little differently, a few specific fingerprints should be left behind to mark a run-through with excellence and efficiency.

Make It Count

It's unsettling how easily this precious prep time can become a goof-off fest. I don't know about you, but I've never felt so over-prepared that I could afford to slack off on my one and only shot through the lesson. Adopt an ethic that says, "I take this time seriously. I'm about to lay my offering on the altar of God."

'Cuz it's true. You are.

Keep Going …

… unless the room leader or teacher (or whoever calls the shots) stops. It takes discipline to keep going when someone messes up a line or when the band starts "Every Move I Make" in the wrong key. But you know what? Pretend the kids are in the room and keep going anyway. This is a great discipline to adopt that helps cement the lesson and "work through" rough patches. It imparts value and professionalism to the work that is highly contagious and lets everyone in the room know "We mean business." You want more value from the higher-ups like the senior pastor? Show the pastor a team at work with a disciplined professional run-through ethic.

WHOOSH!

Focus on the Details

Particularly the transitions. By the time you get to the run-through, the teacher has rehearsed, the actors (if you have any) have done their thing, the music leader has worked his or her fingers across the strings. Only the tech person hasn't had a real shot at this thing. Lights, mics, videos. And while well-run tech really adds to a dynamic creative lesson, clunky tech does nothing but distract. No matter that your tech may be as simple as dimming the room lights and turning on the track lighting that points at the front of the room — make that transition count.

During the run-through, try not to stop the lesson *except* for a tech cue, (like when you spend 37 seconds waiting for that video to cue up or when the teacher is talking but the lights are still dark ... you know, *those* little details). Quickly and efficiently back up to just before the cue and do it again. Yes, it will take the techie a moment to re-cue the video or reset the lights, but this is time well-spent to get it right. This is what the run-through is for: getting through the whole lesson and smoothing out those remaining rough edges along the way. Don't rush through this stuff. Don't be afraid to stop and back up. Details count.

PRACTIS MAKS PURFECT
PRACTICE MAKS PERFERF
PRACTICE MAKES P

Be Consistent

Do a run-through every single weekend. Beyond making the lesson excellent and setting you (and other volunteers) up to win, a big part of all this is about vision. The vision you're casting is this: "The work we do in this ministry is the biggest deal happening in this whole church. We aren't putting on little skits for kids. We are in the life-changing, world-rocking business! All systems go!" All that vision packed into a little thing like a run-through? Believe it.

~~~~~~

Rehearsal works. It builds confidence. It radiates vision. It creates significant and transformational lessons that draw kids closer to God. And it sends the excellence of your ministry soaring like a flying monkey over any local production of *The Wizard of Oz*. And if the high school music teacher happens to bring her kids to your church, sees the quality of the Sunday school teaching, and turns witch-green with envy ...?

Well, that can't be helped.

I'm a bit of a video game maniac. It's probably because of my innately childlike heart. Or maybe I feel a need to research these games for the sake of the boys that I teach on Sundays.

Or maybe I'm just a total über-geek.

So when my son Ethan reached the age of ascension (which I decided was about six or seven), I passed on the legacy to him. Okay, it wasn't so much a legacy as a game controller. I taught him how to outwit Lurkers and outmaneuver enemy hover-bikes in *Jak and Daxter.* I showed him how to defeat the third level boss in *Luigi's Mansion.* We even have our initials in the second-place slot of the *Gauntlet* machine at the water park where we often vacation. Twenty dollars in quarters is a small price to pay for such prestige.

But then it happened. The day came that I always knew must come, but dreaded just the same.

He started to get better than me.

It happened quite suddenly during a heart-pounding two-player session of *MarioKart Double Dash.* I was racing as Princess Peach in the PeachMobile (at the request of my watching daughter, thank you very much), and Ethan was racing as Mario in his tricked-out Mario-Kart. By the time we came out of the hairpin turn at the end of the third lap, it was clear: He was leaving me in the dust. By the end of the race, he had come in first and I was trailing in a pathetic seventh place.

A fluke. Surely.

But over the next hour, my son showed the same proficiency at defending elven woodlands. And saving distant galaxies.

There was no doubt about it. My baby was all grown up and whooping aliens all by himself. And he was giving me pointers.

über-geek

"Dad, if you hold down the R and L buttons for three seconds it gives you a boost of speed." He was miming the proper finger combination in thin air.

"Dad, you have to do a forward roll jump over that pit or you'll fall into the lava." There was sincere concern in his voice. Maybe a little pity.

"Dad, these robots are too fast; you have to use your force field. Here Dad, let me show you." I had been relieved of my controller.

Humbling? Uh, yeah.

I was being schooled by an eight-year-old. Me. A guy who had played the original tabletop version of *Space Invaders* at the dawn of the video game era. A graduate from the prestigious ranks of Atari, Intellivision, and the ever-popular Commodore 64. A veteran of 28 years of video game playing.

But there was one thing I couldn't deny. With my son's patient evaluation and encouragement ... I was getting better. It's not like I stunk to begin with. But, turns out, there was room for improvement.

NOT LIKE THAT, DAD!

Evaluation isn't about saying, "You stink. Let me help you not stink."

Sounds silly, but a lot of us think about evaluation that way. But this formative feedback isn't just about fixing what's broken. It's about growth. It's about being better, more dynamic, more impactful than I am right now. In children's ministry, we have some fear wrapped around this concept. I understand that. Evaluation can seem like scary stuff. Many of us equate feedback with failure. And yet evaluation, when it's done consistently and done well, can be

glub glub

an uplifting experience that spurs us on to greater heights of power and proficiency.

Who among us wouldn't like to consistently rock the room when we teach? To regularly partner in Holy Spirit moments that rattle the walls and leave us breathless?

These are extremely achievable goals, but it takes *development*. I'll bet my antique Atari joystick that when most of us first started teaching creative lessons to kids, we felt like we were in over our heads. We needed development. That is the goal of evaluation. Not criticism. Not just fixing the broken parts. But ongoing and uplifting *development*.

Leaders play an important part in this whole evaluation thing. But they don't hold all the keys. The ownership of evaluation also sits solidly on us teachers.

To be humble.

To authentically long for growth and development.

To look leaders square in the eye and call evaluation out of them.

It requires that we say to our leaders: *"I want to be a better, more powerful, more effective teacher a year from now than I am today. And I'm not going to just drift there by accident. I want you to help me get there. I need you to help me grow through evaluation."*

Overcoming the scary side of evaluation is half the battle. But Jim Marshall and his team at Quest Community Church in Lexington, Kentucky, swallowed their fears and faced evaluation head-on.

"[The idea of evaluation] was avoided in the past because we didn't want to discourage the teacher who had to teach the lesson two more times," said Jim. But his team discovered that their fears were unfounded.

"We found that more encouragement happens in the scheduled evaluation time rather than discouragement. The stakes are so high. This may be the only shot we have with a child, so it's got to be clear, it's got to be engaging, it's got to be transformational. If I have a chance to change [my delivery of the lesson], I will ... so I can reach that child during the next service."

Once the issue of evaluation is out in the open and everyone is speaking the same language, evaluation becomes easy. From there, it's a matter of setting up a consistent approach to evaluation that works for your team, and establishing some rules of play that will help your team master the art of evaluation.

A CONSISTENT APPROACH

What does an evaluation look like?

It's a consistent sit-down meeting with you (the teacher) and one other person—your evaluator. This evaluator could be your ministry director or another teacher. It might be a volunteer you recruit with this specific purpose in mind, someone with strong upfront chops. It might be a handpicked small-group leader whose opinion you especially respect. Bottom line—you're looking for someone with the ability to watch your lesson and give you specific, growth-oriented feedback.

Once you have your evaluation buddy, success requires consistency. Otherwise, evaluation can easily turn into a "hit or miss" deal. One week, your evaluator is a no-show, and you find her doling out fish crackers in the understaffed toddler room like feeding time at the seal pit. That's a problem. In no time, your weekly critique has eroded into a "make-a-comment-only-when-something-is-broken" approach. Before you know what hit you, you're back to interpreting any feedback as a character assassination. And let's face it … that's the opposite of helpful.

Remember, the goal of evaluation is ongoing and uplifting development of your skills. Set a consistent standing

brrrr! cold.

43° below zero

Hey, a page with no art. What gives?!

appointment with your evaluation buddy to discuss your lesson every week. This isn't a "chat-while-walking-down-the-hall-eating-a-bagel-and-checking-your-voicemail" kind of conversation. There's a proper time and place for that kind of intense multitasking, like when you're driving your car. But it won't serve you well for an evaluation of your teaching. Sit down somewhere relatively quiet and do a proper face-to-face. Give yourself a full 20 minutes for nothing but a solid and clear evaluation.

You always say you want more time for yourself, right? This 20 minutes is all about you. Go on. Enjoy it.

IS THIS A GOOD TIME?

You could hold this evaluation time during the weekend, directly after the service when both you and your evaluator are already there. But you could also wait until later in the week when the chaos of the weekend is over and you have more perspective about the weekend. The danger in waiting is that after a couple days we tend to be romantically optimistic in our recollection of what actually occurred. It's easy to forget that the moment when you parted the Red Sea wasn't really as magical as you had hoped. Or that the kids unraveled into an angry torch-bearing mob during the game show. (Remember when they set fire to the stage? Ahh ... memories.) It may be better to stick around on the weekend when your memory is fresh and honest.

For many ministries, the weekend involves more than one service. If that is true in your setting, then evaluation takes on an additional role. Not only are you focused on the ongoing development of your skills, but it becomes important to assess the first service and decide if anything needs to change for subsequent services. If something goofy happened in the first service (you misquoted Scripture, for example) or some element of the lesson clearly didn't work (angry torch-bearing mob, remember?), there's no sense repeating the same mistakes again. An ideal time for evaluation is after the first service. I know that turn-around times between services are tight, so you'll have to be creative. If your ministry incorporates small groups, you and your evaluator might huddle up then, while kids are in their small groups. This gives you time to make any slight adjustments before hurtling into the next service.

RULES OF PLAY

Before you hit the gas on evaluation, it's critical to get everyone in the same lane. Some rules of the road help. In a game where feedback is part of play, clear expectations go a long way to making your evaluation powwows successful.

Here are some ground rules both teachers and evaluators can use to grease the wheels of the evaluation game.

Teachers

⭐ **Agree to take an active role in evaluation.** This means asking questions and seeking improvement. You are an active and willing participant, not a critique victim who's on the verge of relegating your evaluation buddy to bad-guy status.

⭐ **Commit to short-term growth *and* long-term development.** If you have multiple services on the weekend, strive to make each service better than the last. But also give laser-focus to improving specific techniques and skills over the long haul, knowing that your evaluation huddle provides a consistent and safe place to check your progress.

⭐ **Humbly welcome the benefit of accountability and support.** Remember, this isn't *your* Sunday school class, much as it may feel like it—you are part of a team. Even if you work solo with your room of kids each week, chances are that there are leaders, whether staff or volunteer, that oversee the ministry. You are accountable to your leaders for what gets taught … and you need to be supported by them along the way. Go team.

* **Free yourself from having to please everybody.** Because your work happens to be on display for all to see, for some weird reason everybody and their sister finds it a perfectly acceptable practice to come up and offer their opinions about what you should have done differently in the lesson. Small group leaders. Parents. Well-meaning strangers. Stray dogs. You name it. Feedback from too many voices is far from helpful. In fact, it can breed insecurity and doubt. You start to think it's your job to make everyone happy, to change your lesson to address every comment. No more. In the context of evaluation, you now have a safe and consistent place to bounce ideas around, get feedback, and make team decisions about what, if any, changes need to be made.

Evaluators

* **Commit to consistency.** In the hurly-burly of a busy weekend, it's easy for a leader to become distracted by other matters. But this is one get-together that leaders (or other designated evaluation buddy) can't blow off. It's important to uphold the value and importance of providing an intentional and consistent vehicle for growth.

* **Put the positive first.** In every lesson, there are things that rock and things that reek. It's important for evaluators to view this feedback powwow as a time and place to encourage as well as challenge and mentor teachers. Evaluators earn the right to comment on the "growth opportunities" by pointing out the good stuff first.

* **Focus on two types of correction.** There's correction that focuses on long-term development. And then there's immediate "fix-it-before-the-next-service" types of changes. A teacher's

long-term growth should be dead-center in the crosshairs. Evaluation's prime purpose is development. But in a church where multiple services are part of the reality, immediate changes need to be kept in the sights as well, so subsequent services can reap the rewards.

Be specific. Saying "that was good" is just no good. General comments like this don't do squat to encourage and develop a growing teacher. Comments need to be as detailed as possible, focusing on specifics of technique and skill.

- **General:** "That was really good. I liked it."
- **Specific:** "Did you feel the momentum of the lesson when you drove your pacing and energy forward to Goliath's defeat? They were cheering for David … and then you stopped everything and went silent … and you could hear a pin drop. You turned the corner, you slowly and methodically laid out the application, and the kids were putty in your hand. Rock on! Now, let's look at

THAT'S REALLY GREAT! NEXT TIME REMEMBER TO JUMP UP AND DOWN TO REALLY SCARE THEM the beginning of the lesson … when you asked for responses to your question, they all unraveled…. let's work on that."

Feel the difference? Specific comments simultaneously encourage and equip, high-fiving a teacher's success and equipping for exciting new moments of success.

✱ **Create a safe context for growth and accountability.** There's a reason having a consistent evaluator is so important. Trust. Pushing themselves to new heights is risky for teachers; it sometimes involves taking chances and occasionally falling flat. Teachers need to know that their evaluation buddies are in their corner, cheering them on and setting them up to soar. Evaluators need to keep the big picture in mind, making sure teachers have a safe environment in which to try new things while not letting them off the hook when it comes to keeping skills moving on an upward trajectory.

EVALUATING YOUR OPTIONS

What if no one is available to evaluate creative teaching? What if leaders feel ill-equipped to provide meaningful feedback? No sweat. Consider these options.

Peer Evaluation

Buddy up with another teacher and watch each other on your off weekends. Or gather all the teachers together as a group sometime midweek for a little feedback fiesta. This makes a kickin' party for comments, development, and cheering each other on. Bonus feature: while you're trading tips and dipping chips, you'll pick up some new

somebody say FIESTA???

me bring SALSA! ME LOVE SALSA!!

ideas from each other and become more of a unified creative team along the way.

Video Evaluation

Click on the camera. Even a camcorder on a tripod at the back of the room provides a valuable self-evaluation tool. Review this on your own, or bring it to your feedback fiesta with all the teachers. You can each take turns viewing and critiquing each other's video. Nothing brings a team together like watching your Joshua lesson in high-definition surround sound.

Comparative Evaluation

Not sure you have words to evaluate someone else or yourself? Wondering what the bulls-eye looks like? Nothing clarifies the target like having an example. Luckily, there are several good videos and DVDs out there that highlight solid creative teaching. Pick up some of these (try the Promiseland Curriculum videos, Saddleback videos, and Kidmo videos for starters … you can search these out on the web with a quick Google), and try to identify great teaching in action. Pick them apart as a teaching team and discuss what dynamic teaching looks like for your ministry.

STAYING TRUE TO FORM

Okay, I'm not a big one for using a checklist-style evaluation form. Using forms feels kind of like cramming a painting into a mathematical equation or reducing a complex craft into a quick-and-easy to-do list. However, as a shout-out to the loads of teachers who have asked for a

SALSA SALSA SALSA EVERYBODY invited!!!!!!

resource like this, I've included one in the appendix (pages 298–299). Hear me loud and clear—this form is not a report card. Rating teachers on a 1-out-of-10 scale or giving them grades is a no-no in my book. Throws off the mojo. Instead, think of this form as a guide … a jumping off point … a springboard … a roadmap … pick your analogy … to help you score big with the awesome art of evaluation.

Turns out my video game skills aren't the only things under evaluation. While goofing around with my son the other day, he informed me that my armpit farts need work. Personally, I thought I had my technique down cold.

On the other hand, maybe some things are better left unevaluated.

Strategy. Structure. And spiders.

The stuff of nightmares.

I don't scare easily, but these three S-words have been a severe source of the willies for me as long as I can remember. And while I've been able to keep my life fairly spider free by avoiding arachnid hangouts like the woods and my basement, when it came to strategy and structure, I finally had to face my fear head on.

NOTICE
NO SKATEBOARDING
NO ROLLERBLADING
NO LOITERING
and most of all...
NO SKIPPING THIS CHAPTER

If you're creatively inclined like me, a discussion of ministry structure may fill you with dread. You may relegate such a strategic discussion to a "leaders only" domain, and be tempted to skip this chapter and move on. Enticing, I know. The terror runs deep. But I urge you to resist the impulse.

Is this a chapter for ministry leaders? Kinda.

SPACE FOR SALE

Developers of book on Sunday school techniques offering approximately 3/5 of page to interested buyer. Content must be wholesome. Preferably Sunday school related. Non smoker. Some spiders on next page.

stuff of nightmares?
hey, that ME!

But it's also a chapter for you. For teachers who recognize that they are uniquely positioned to influence the direction of the ministry. For teachers who realize that a smart and strategic teaching rotation can be a key ingredient in making practices like memorization, rehearsal, and evaluation possible.

Icky? Maybe at first. But undeniable. So let's dive right into the administrative guts of it.

Structurally speaking, we all have to set up some system for rotating volunteer teachers. Especially if your ministry conducts more than one service on Sunday. But how we set up that rotation strategy is a major factor in creating a healthy environment — one that allows excellence to develop, minimizes burnout, and equips teachers for ongoing development.

THAT KID OF OURS WONT CATCH A SINGLE FLY WITHOUT SOME BASIC STRUCTURE AND STRATEGY.

MM, GOOD FLY-CUPCAKE, HON.

So let's give some eyeball time to three possibilities. Three different rotation strategies, each with their own set of pros and cons. For the sake of these sample structures, let's assume your children's ministry teaches all of your elementary kids in a combined K–5 teaching time. If you break into grade-specific groupings, just explode the model out (not literally please). Let's also assume that you have three services on the weekend ... a 9:00 a.m., a 10:30 a.m., and a 12:00 noon. Again, this is just to get us off and running and not meant to reflect every reality. Adjust as needed.

THE ONE-SERVICE APPROACH

The one-service rotation structure is commonly used in children's ministries. It looks like this:

ONE-SERVICE APPROACH

Kindergarten—Fifth Grade

9:00 a.m. Service Teacher 1	10:30 a.m. Service Teacher 2	12:00 noon Service Teacher 3

In this approach, three different teachers (or teaching teams) teach the exact same lesson at a different service every week. One teacher does the 9:00 a.m. service, another does the 10:30 a.m. service (exact same lesson!), and a third does the 12:00 noon service (also the exact same lesson!) Sound familiar? Maybe, maybe not, but check out the pros and cons of this way of working.

Pros

- **Looks good.** The perception, at first glance anyway, is that this is a manageable, bite-sized serving commitment. After all, it's only one service a week, right? It doesn't shake out that way in the long run, however. Check out the cons.

Cons

- **Wasted time.** In other words, if Teacher 1 spends five hours a week prepping his lesson, so do Teacher 2 and Teacher 3. Preparing the exact same lesson! That's ten hours wasted repeating work that's already being done. No wonder you don't have time to ... umm ... memorize or rehearse.

- **High burnout factor.** The truth of the matter? Although it looks good at first glance, the work required of this commitment is a hard grind. Teaching every single weekend is draining, especially in light of the prep time involved. This whopper-sized commitment week after week can quickly lead to inconsistency (not showing up as faithfully), burnout (feeling crispy around the edges), and eventually dropout (running screaming into the night). Hmmm ... this may not be a recipe for excellent and sustainable ministry.

- **No lessons learned between services.** Teacher 2 shows up cold for the second service, without the benefit of all those hard-won lessons Teacher 1 learned during the 9:00 service. Lessons like "don't do the audience interaction section after the Bible story because the little heathens completely unravel and come close to staging a mutiny." Helpful stuff like that.

  Imagine getting a chance to improve and grow the lesson —and your skills—over the weekend! Well, with the one-service approach, you can forget it. It can't happen when the guard changes at the second service.

- **Limited gift and skill development.** It's discouraging to put so much preparation into a lesson and get only one run at it. Not only do you often leave on Sunday feeling like you didn't really move the ball up the field very much, but the long-term skill development of a model like this leaves a lot to be desired.

If this approach feels frighteningly familiar, don't worry. First, weigh out those pros and cons. Determine whether your rotation structure may be inhibiting you from achieving optimal excellence.

Are there other options? Yes indeedy.

THE WHOLE-WEEKEND APPROACH

Imagine if you will, a different teaching rotation. One that allows time for memorization and practice. One that builds balance into teachers lives, ensuring long-term sustainability. One that ... oh, forget imagining, just take a look at this:

THE WHOLE-WEEKEND APPROACH

Kindergarten—Fifth Grade

	9:00 a.m. Service	10:30 a.m. Service	12:00 noon Service	
Weekend 1	Teacher 1	Teacher 1	Teacher 1	
Weekend 2	Teacher 2	Teacher 2	Teacher 2	
Weekend 3	Teacher 3	Teacher 3	Teacher 3	
Weekend 4	Teacher 4	Teacher 4	Teacher 4	

Nope, you're not reading it upside down. It really says to have each teacher teach the entire weekend. Don't jump to any conclusions yet ... let's do our whole pros and cons thing first.

Cons

● **Teacher misses the adult service one week out of four.** That is, if your children's ministry runs simultaneous to the adult service. True, the teacher who's up for the weekend misses the weekend service for big people. But that's why God created CDs. Seriously, it's been my experience that being freed up for three weeks solid to simply attend and worship, rather than gearing up every weekend for the whole serve-and-attend marathon, really pays off. Teachers feel *more* connected with the weekend services, not less. And don't forget the amount of time that's been freed up to pour into the lesson on your *on* weekend. Teachers go much deeper in preparing their lessons, which, quite frankly, becomes a teaching and worship experience in itself.

Pros

- **On for one weekend, off for three!** Admit it, once you get used to the idea, it sounds blissful, doesn't it? Truth is, it really is a more fulfilling and bite-sized commitment.
- **Strategic use of volunteer time.** No more wasted hours spent prepping up the exact same lessons. This frees you teachers to go deeper during your *on* weekend (meaning rehearsal and memorization), which leads to greater excellence and more powerful teaching.
- **Sustainability.** This is doable for the long haul. After teaching multiple services, you leave at the end of the weekend feeling tired (I mean, let's be honest), but you'll also feel *so* much more fulfilled. You start to really catch a clear vision that you aren't just helping out in the children's ministry but that you are in the life-changing business. Which you are. And don't you forget it.
- **The services get better and better.** Yep. Each service grows because the teacher is learning along the way. By the noon service, you're cooking with gas.
- **Skills jump forward by leaps.** There's something about digging into a lesson and taking it across the finish line that really lets you flex your skills and put them to the test. While you may be doing only 12 lessons a year (rather than 52 ... scary when you put it like that, isn't it?), the depth in those 12 lessons is exponentially richer and the potential for growing your gift is so much more tangible.

THE WHOLE-UNIT APPROACH

I'm all about options, so here's one more structure model to think about. While this approach isn't ideal for everybody, it can be extremely effective if your curriculum breaks the lessons into four-week units.

THE WHOLE-UNIT APPROACH

Kindergarten—Fifth Grade

Unit 1 (four weeks)	**Teacher 1** All three services for all four weeks	
Unit 2 (four weeks)	**Teacher 2** All three services for all four weeks	
Unit 3 (four weeks)	**Teacher 3** All three services for all four weeks	

Cons

- **Teacher misses the adult service four weeks straight.** Yep, I get it. Again, CDs are an option. You have to determine whether or not something like this can work in your church's culture. Remember, teachers get to go to the adult service two months straight, distraction free.
- **Four weekends straight is a lot.** Maybe, maybe not. Again, you have to take the temperature on your culture. In some ministries, a serving commitment like this is no sweat; in others … it's a harder pill for us teachers to swallow.

58

Pros

In addition to all of the benefits from the second model (strategic use of volunteer time, sustainability, the services get better and better, skills jump forward by leaps), this structure has these pros as well:

- **On for one month, off for two!** Teachers often really love the break that this model affords them and feel like they can serve year round because of it. It totals up to 16 weeks *on*, and 24 weeks *off* per year.

- **High ownership of lesson units.** The teachers I talk to who use this model say they love having complete ownership of the whole unit. They are thrilled they get to dig in and go deep.

- **More time to prep.** Again, teachers love the amount of time they have to prep up units and get ready for their *on* unit. In terms of excellence, you'll find it brings your whole game up several notches.

- **Cohesive units.** This often translates into units of lessons that feel pulled together and have a common thread. You don't have other teachers trying to make sense of lesson groupings that go together when they weren't there on weeks 1 and 2. This means stronger, more cohesive teaching, and more effective themes.

The Whole-Unit Approach may seem a little extreme at first glance, especially if you're part of a smaller church. It's not for everybody. But I've worked with many ministries that love it. Denise Dyer at Grace Community Church in Columbia, Maryland, told me: "It has transformed our ministry. The teachers began to really own what they were doing. They saw the impact of their teaching because they knew what happened last week and the week before. They were in the know! When their unit started they were charged with energy. They had just had 8 weeks off to plan and get excited!"

All her teachers agree. Food for thought.

FOOD?! somebody say FOOOOD?!

As a teacher in Sunday school, you may feel like it's just your job to show up and do the weekend … that these strategic issues are the domain of leadership. But you are a major stakeholder in the ministry! This is your ministry! Offer to meet with your leaders for the purpose of creating and implementing the kinds of strategic changes that will transform the ministry into an atmosphere of excellence. Talk about your options. Take a new teaching rotation for a two-month test drive. Don't be afraid to bring strategic-minded issues like this to your leaders' attention.

Somewhere along my journey down the fabulous path of children's ministry, I realized that, as a Sunday school teacher, I needed to partner with the leaders of my ministry to shape a strong and dynamic teaching structure that would create a thriving environment for excellence. And while my fear of eight-legged creepy-crawlies remains as paralyzing as ever, I wholeheartedly embrace the power of a solid rotation structure.

Just don't ask me to look at the budget. Not unless you want to see a grown man scream like a little girl.

PART TWO

Fabulous
Techniques
for

Transformational
Teaching

I'm not much of a baker. Don't get me wrong, I can cook. But baking's not my thing. So when my daughter's birthday comes along and I need a cake, I do what many of us do these days. I run down to the supermarket and buy one.

I know that if I just took a little time to learn some basics of cake-making techniques, then I'd never have to worry about another cake crisis again. The techniques would serve me whether I needed a birthday cake or a dessert for Christmas dinner. Chocolate, vanilla, or carrot, those are just slight adjustments when you have some cake technique under your apron.

Since I don't aspire to be a world-class cake baker, I'll probably continue to make my last-minute supermarket runs when confronted with a cake emergency.

But I *do* aspire to be a dynamic teacher of transformational Bible lessons. And, I'm guessing, so do you.

New activities. Coloring pages. Conversation starters. These common ministry stopgaps are like that run to the market … they provide a quick teaching fix, but none of them take your teaching to powerful new levels. Even a good curriculum, though very helpful, is not the silver bullet.

But techniques … truly creative teaching techniques … these serve you over the long haul. It doesn't matter whether your lesson is about Jonah or Jesus; from a store-bought curriculum or one you wrote yourself; for kindergartners or fifth-graders. With some practical teaching techniques, you'll be ready for transformation.

Some of the techniques in this section focus on the planning process. Others are specific to upfront delivery. But all the techniques set you on a path of true development, taking your technique toward transformational.

And the thrill that comes from seeing yourself develop and grow … the excitement of seeing the kids suddenly respond in whole new ways … the sheer exhilaration of having your new-found techniques take the whole ministry to new heights … well, it's better than a second serving of Death by Chocolate.

CHAPTER 5

PLANNING POWERFUL PROGRAMS

Sunday has a nasty habit of showing up every seven days. It's kind of like your crazy cousin Otto, who visits far more often than he should, eats everything in the fridge, makes a few long distance phone calls, leaves the house trashed, and disappears, only to show up again a week later.

Most of us love Sunday. We truly do. Yet we can't help wishing that, like Otto, it would visit with a little less regularity.

When it comes to taking the bite out of the weekly grind of children's ministry, planning is an essential ingredient to ridding ourselves of the pressure-induced pinch. Whether your planning process involves brainstorming and writing your curriculum from scratch, giving a nip and tuck to a store-bought curriculum, or simply printing the lesson pages from a tried-and-true curriculum you've used for years, a little planning can relax away some of those worry lines and ensure that you arrive on Sunday sane, with the most dynamic lesson possible.

GETTING AHEAD OF THE GAME

One of the best gifts you can give yourself is to plan lessons at least four weeks ahead. Just like sucking the helium out of an overly taut balloon, you can relieve a great amount of pressure (not to mention the giddy, lightheaded feeling you might experience) when you spend *this* week writing, adapting, or planning the lesson that will be taught ... not this Sunday ... but the Sunday *four weeks* from now.

I can feel the stress melting away already.

So ... how do you get onto this wonderful path of planning ahead, and out of the seven-day spin-cycle? I'd be lying if I said it was a

Dude, got anything in your fridge?

PLANNING

WEEK 2 WEEK 3

WEEK 1 WEEK 4

piece of cake. It requires taking a break from the grind for the purpose of pulling ahead. Taking a break from the usual teaching routine allows you to pour more horsepower into planning and prepping lessons for the coming weeks.

That's great, you say. *But how?*

Pushy, pushy, pushy. Here are some strategies to mull over in the great quest for advanced planning.

Option 1

Try this on for option 1: Work ahead during the slower summer months. Or if your summer tends to be no slower than any other time of the year, intentionally schedule a different kind of summer to allow a little wiggle room. That might mean doing a simpler, less intensive program this summer or saying no to something like VBS for one year. A tough bullet for some of us to bite, I know. But in the battle for advanced planning (which leads to powerful lessons and a little thing I like to call *sanity*), something's gotta give. The payoff is worth it.

Option 2

Consider dividing up the team to conquer the time crunch, with part of the team working several weeks out while the others temporarily pull double duty. If you're currently split into grade-specific break-downs, like grades K–2 and 3–5, consider combining them both into

K–5 for one month. Half the teachers go on "lesson development duty" while the others cover the weekends. In one month, at a rate of one lesson per week, a single teacher could get the team ahead by four weeks. Two teachers on lesson prep detail could get you eight weeks out. Imagine how different life could be in the long-term by combining efforts for one month.

Option 3

Okay … dare I say it? It's crazy talk, I know … but maybe you put a great DVD series in front of the kids for four weeks. It's not a sin, you know. Trust me, I looked it up. During this month of "canned programming," all the teachers can come together to form a SWAT team for lesson prep. Lots of us cringe at the prospect of just pressing play on a video, myself included, but let's face it … no kid's going to go to hell because you put in *VeggieTales* for a month. If it gives you the elbow room you need to build some breathing space into the ministry,

then it sounds like a pretty

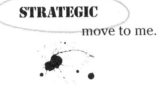

STRATEGIC

move to me.

However you get four weeks ahead, this type of planning brings great intentionality and power to your lessons, not to mention relieving a boatload of stress-induced headaches. Build in a weekly meeting

to look at lessons together (together can mean you and your leader, or a bigger get-together with teachers from other grade levels or rotations). This will keep some accountability in the mix. Have weekly deadlines during this getting-ahead time to keep the train on the tracks. And while you're planning those lessons with a little more breathing room and a little less pressure, here are some principles to bear in mind that will help your lessons be well on their way toward powerful long before Sunday ever shows up.

LEARNING STYLES 101

The concept of learning styles absolutely upended my approach to teaching kids. The long explanation about learning styles is ... well ... long. And way past the scope of this book. If you want the nuts and bolts about learning styles, pick up a great book by Cynthia Ulrich Tobias called *The Way They Learn*.

But here's the Cliffs Notes version:

Kids learn in primarily three different ways. And while many kids process information in a combination of ways, most will have one dominant learning style. Auditory. Visual. Or kinesthetic.

That's learning styles in a nutshell. That's it. That's the big Aha. Simple, isn't it? And yet, Monday through Friday, most schools continue to pelt kids with information in primarily one way. By talking.

But talking is mostly an auditory teaching method. So consequently, talking only speaks clearly to some of the kids in the crowd. Meanwhile, kids who learn best in other ways are left hanging on by their fingernails until **RECESS**,

or the occasional filmstrip about *honeybees*,

or the field trip to the SCIENCE MUSEUM,

or **something** ...

anything ... that will speak their language.

KA-PING!

The auditory kids are easy to pick out of the lineup … they're often the ones who sit still in their seats, taking good notes, listening to every word the teacher says … the ones teachers consider the *good kids*. Most teaching methods are designed with auditory kids in mind.

But listen up. While statistics on learning styles are tricky to find, one study conducted and recorded in *Engineering Education* magazine found that students retain only 10 percent of what they read, 26 percent of what they hear, 30 percent of what they see, 50 percent of what they see and hear, 70 percent of what they say, and 90 percent of what they say as they do something. Whatever else this study may tell us, it lets us know that most students (kids included) don't learn best by simply being talked at. Sadly, while kids are regularly barraged with an avalanche of talk, talk, talk, the cold silent truth is … most kids aren't auditory learners.

*10%?
THAT'S
NOT
MUCH*

*↗
90% —
MUCH
BETTER*

For visual kids, seeing is believing. They're the ones that perk up when the video starts and stare out the window when hour number three of the droning lecture-fest rolls around.

Kinesthetic learners? Sitting at a desk for hours on end is the kinesthetic learner's equivalent of Chinese water torture. Is your son's midterm progress report riddled with comments like: "Jimmy fidgets too much" or "Jimmy talks to his neighbor too much" or "Jimmy can't seem to keep his hands to himself"?

Bingo. Kinesthetic learner alert.

So …

*VISUAL
KID
↓*

What's the shiny little nugget at the end of the learning styles rainbow?

What's the pearl in the learning styles oyster?

What's the diamond in the learning styles coal mine?

What's the … sorry. Moving on.

*AUDITORY
LEARNER*

Those are ears, by the w

Here's my major learning about learning styles: When planning powerful programs, hit *every* learning style in *every lesson*. I'm not just doing a Bible talk-a-thon for the auditory angels. I want those visual kids to know I pictured the lesson with them in mind. I want the squirmers and shakers to soar when it comes to understanding who God is. No exceptions.

Want a lesson that will make eyes pop for visual kids?

Try visual storytelling techniques.

Put props in the mix.

Press play on video clips.

Break out the paints for an art attack.

Instead of just saying the verse, use PowerPoint or make a funky chalkboard verse display like one of those coffee-house menu boards.

Every time you shift out of *telling* the kids about the Bible teaching and into *showing* the kids the Bible teaching, you paint a power-packed picture for all those visual learners out there. So make sure *every lesson* you serve up is chock-a-block with it's FDA recommended weekend allowance of visual methods.

Want to find your kinesthetic groove?

A good game show fits the bill nicely.

Take questions from kids in the audience.

Get things moving with audience participation methods.

Work things out with high-energy worship.

Local Man Discovers Kinesthetic Groove

Anything that gets the kids physically involved as they experience the Bible will help those truths hit them where it counts.

What about auditory? No worries. You're already hitting the auditory learners just by flapping your lips.

THE RULE OF THREE

When it comes to planning powerful programs, creativity is key. And while different rules apply to the preschool crowd (check out chapter 10), I always want to keep elementary-aged kids guessing. So when I'm writing a new lesson or giving an existing lesson a minor overhaul, I live by a little guideline called The Rule of Three.

Don't worry. Despite its name, The Rule of Three involves no math … well, no hard math. And while it may smack slightly of counting up points to you Weight Watchers alums out there, I assure you that the counting involved in this planning regimen is pain free. Simply put, use at least three different creative methods in every lesson. And talking doesn't count as a creative method. Maybe in law school, but not in children's ministry.

Any of the creative methods explored in Part 3 of this book count toward your final score of three.

Game Show? Counts.
Audience Participation? Counts.
Visual Props? Counts.
Talking? Don't even.

In addition to the methods from Part 3, any other creative support methods I can think of get points in the tally. Video. Drama. Puppets. Music. Any one of these gets credit toward that three-point count.

When you're gearing up for that lesson on The Last Supper, bravo for bringing 12 kids up around the table and using them for audience participation.

Audience Participation … that's one. But don't towel off quite yet.

After you get that story told, follow it up with a simple game show that lets kids give modern-day examples of a foot-washing-style service that they can live out.

Game Show for the application ... that's two.

Then drive it home with a worship time that rocks the house.

Worship ... you just hit creative method three. Way to go! Hit the showers.

THE APPLICATION FACTOR

Have you ever wondered why God chose to include certain stories in the Bible? I mean, lots of other stuff happened. Stuff that isn't in there. So why handpick Gideon out for publication? Why include the story of Joshua and Jericho instead of some other long-forgotten battle? Why the story of Esther but not the story of Bubba? (I'm just speculating that there might have been a Bubba in the mix somewhere along the way ... don't hold me to that.) Why these stories?

I have a theory. It's not some deep theologically researched thesis. It hasn't been corroborated in some lost text written by the apostle Paul. It's just a guess. A hunch, really.

It goes like this: I don't believe the story of Gideon is about Gideon. Yes, it's a real story. Yes, it really happened. But if that's where it stops, then the Bible is just a great history book with a God twist. I believe that the story of Gideon is not, in fact, a story about Gideon. I believe it's a story about me. And about you. And about the kids you teach.

The stories in the Bible have the power to transform the way I follow God. They inherently possess the power to change my life and the way I do life. If this is true, if I really believe this, then it changes the way I plan for Sunday. Because, in light of these thoughts, I'm no longer free to just teach a biblical history and call it a day. It's not enough for me to cram a verse into little Sarah's short-term memory and reward her with a plastic spider ring for reciting it to me the following week. If I truly believe that the stories and teachings in the Bible have the power to transform little Sarah's life and change the way she does life, then my job is not only to tell her these stories but prep her on how to live them out when she goes to school on Monday.

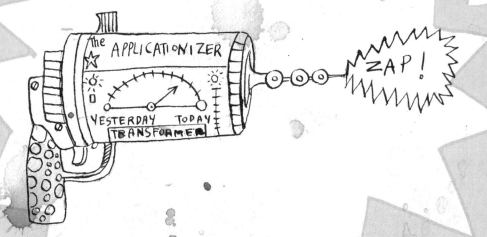

If you're using a ready-made curriculum that has a strong, detailed application already written in—then score! You're good to go! But if you're writing your own lessons, or if you find that your curriculum is weak or devoid of solid application (it's amazing how often the application just isn't there!), then seriously consider adding in the application during the planning stage. Every lesson should answer the application question: Great story ... but so what? What does it have to do with my life? That's what Sarah needs to know. That's why ... among other reasons ... the stories in the Bible are in there.

Application. That's what leads to transformational teaching.

Technique in Action:

-APPLYING GIDEON-

Here's my lesson script for Gideon. This lesson starts with the story. I've jumped in partway through and condensed it ... for your reading pleasure:

So Gideon gathered his army together, which totaled 32,000 men. Now that seems like a lot, but the Midianites had many, many more men. The Bible says the Midianites had more men in their army than the grains of sand on the beach. When Gideon realized this, he was freakin' out. "There's no way my army can beat them," he said.

Even so, early the next morning, God spoke to Gideon. "Even though the other army is bigger, I want you to get rid of some of your men. That way, when you win the battle, you'll know it was me that did it and not yourselves. Tell the men that anyone who is scared can go home."

What? Make the army smaller? That was the last thing Gideon wanted to do. It made no sense ... but he obeyed. When he told the men what God had said, 22,000 men booked it for home.

But God said, "No, still too many men. Take the remaining 10,000 men down to the water for a drink. Those who drink with their hands will stay, but those who bend over on their hands and knees and drink the water like a dog, should go home." Weird directions, but okay. So Gideon did it, even though he didn't want to lose more men. And out of all the men, only 300 drank with their hands. All the rest drank the water like dogs, and were sent home.

So, that night, Gideon led his army of 300 quietly to the edge of the Midianite camp. "Alright, here are God's instructions ... everybody take a glass jar and a trumpet. Surround the camp on all sides, and get your trumpets ready. When I blow my trumpet, break your jars,

CONTINUED!

blow your trumpets and shout." So the 300 men surrounded the camp and when Gideon gave the signal, they all blew their trumpets and shouted as loud as they could "A sword for the Lord and for Gideon!" When the Midianites heard the noise they panicked and were so terrified that they pulled out their swords and destroyed each other. Gideon's army beat the Midianites, and they barely even had to pull out their swords!

Story's been told. Game over, right? No way. Because without application, this story is just so much ancient history. How does the story of Gideon apply to Sarah? What's the one clear walkaway you can give her for this week? Here's mine ...

Get rid of most of the army? Break pottery jars? Yell? That's no way to beat an army. In a tough situation, with weird instructions from God, Gideon just had to give it up and trust.

Here it comes. Time to get personal.

And so ... do ... you.

True ... you're not facing an enemy army this week. Or are you?

Because for some of you girls, school feels like a battlefield every single day. And that clique of cool girls ... you know ... the ones that leave you out ... that make you feel so uncool ...

No prisoners ... I'm hitting them right where it hurts. Because that's where God lives.

... they feel like an enemy army.

As if that isn't enough ... God has weird instructions for you too. Stuff like ... "love your enemy," "make sure you don't pay back wrong for wrong." Those instructions are right there in the Bible.

They don't make sense. That's no way to beat your enemy, right?

Pointed. Personal. Close to home. They're all thinking this ...

But God has victories in store for you ... every bit as spectacular as Gideon's ... if you will just give it up ... the hurt ... the pain ... the need for revenge on those girls ...

CONTINUED!

... and trust.

Now, get specific and tangible. Leave them with the take-home ...

So don't pay back wrong for wrong ... let it go. Give up that need for revenge ... as nasty as they may be to you ... let it go.

Because God has got victory in store for you ... even if you can't see it from where you are right now ... if you will only let it go ...

... if you will only follow his instructions ...

... and trust.

Make sure the application is in every lesson. If it's not, give some real thought to adding it in. Because our job isn't just to tell Sarah the story of Gideon. Our job is to make sure she knows that the story about Gideon ... is a story about Sarah.

THE STYLE MAKEOVER

Regardless of what curriculum you use, every once in a while you'll hit a lesson or unit that feels as stale as that stray chicken McNugget that's hiding on the floorboard of your car. The references feel out of date, the creative method feels tired. Our instinct? Throw the lesson out and start over. But before you shred that lesson, take a good look at the content. If the biblical content is solid, maybe you don't need a do-over. Maybe what the lesson is really crying out for is a style makeover.

a chicken nugget

an old lesson plan that should not have been crumpled up, because the content was solid, it just needed a style makeover

a second nugget!!

A few things found on the floorboards of Aaron's car!

When you run up against those lackluster lessons, ask yourself some gut-level questions about content and style:

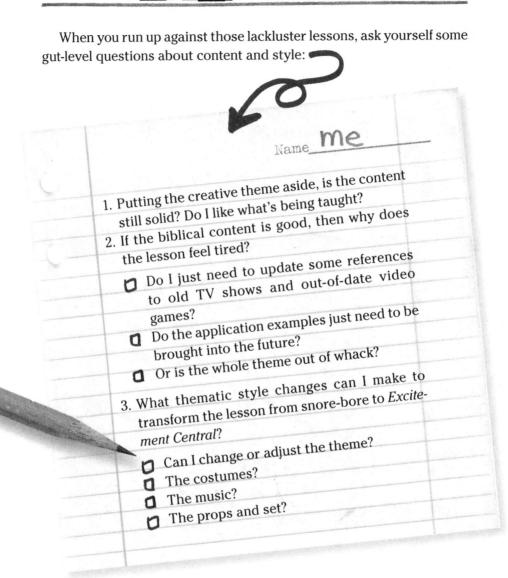

Name **me**

1. Putting the creative theme aside, is the content still solid? Do I like what's being taught?

2. If the biblical content is good, then why does the lesson feel tired?

   ☐ Do I just need to update some references to old TV shows and out-of-date video games?

   ☐ Do the application examples just need to be brought into the future?

   ☐ Or is the whole theme out of whack?

3. What thematic style changes can I make to transform the lesson from snore-bore to *Excitement Central*?

   ☐ Can I change or adjust the theme?
   ☐ The costumes?
   ☐ The music?
   ☐ The props and set?

We're not talking about on-the-fly changes. We're talking about giving the lesson a simple but intentional overhaul by reinventing the style as part of the planning process.

Enough talk about this style stuff ... let's get into the guts of it.

Technique in Action:

The Lesson: *Mission: Unstoppable*.

The Biblical Content: Jesus picks 12 disciples and prepares them for the unstoppable mission of changing the world. Each disciple is introduced by name in a highly memorable, prop-driven way.

The Thematic Style: You guessed it. *Mission: Impossible.* Prerecorded messages that self-destruct, black spy vests, briefcases that contain props associated with each disciple.

The Problem: It feels a little tired. Out of date. Lame.

The Breakdown: After close examination of the lesson, I feel that the biblical content is great. The lesson is a great introduction to the 12 disciples, and it's highly application-oriented, casting a powerful vision to kids that *they* are part of this unstoppable mission to change the world by telling everyone about Jesus. Really good content.

As far as creativity goes, the lesson is wrapped in a spy type of theme, very *Mission: Impossible.* At the time the lesson was created, the movie *Mission: Impossible,* starring Tom Cruise, had just hit screens. The spy theme provided a very current and cool vehicle for teaching this content. But as time goes on, the *Mission: Impossible* references feel tired.

CONTINUED!

YE HAA!

STYLE MAKE OVER

The Solution: Style Makeover.

The Options: A few short years after *Mission: Impossible* hit screens, *The Matrix* was the hottest thing going. So what if the *Mission: Unstoppable* lesson took on a *Matrix* look? Trade out the black spy vests for black trench-coats and shades. That pre-recorded "your mission, should you choose to accept it" tape that we're using to communicate the verse and the application examples ... we could change it out for the all-too-familiar green scrolling binary code on the video screen that kids associate with *The Matrix*. Let's grab some of the music from *The Matrix* soundtrack and use it as a sound bed underneath the lesson. Change a few of the *Mission: Impossible*-esque references to more *Matrix*-y language.

All right, you got me. At the time I'm writing this, even *The Matrix* seems a bit out of touch. Maybe even more so if you're reading this in 2050. No prob. For 2006, I might wrap the whole lesson in a *Spy Kids* approach. Or *Shark Boy and Lava Girl*. Or *Kim Possible*. Anything that lends itself to this whole "Unstoppable Mission" kind of content. In 2050? Who knows? Maybe *Mission: Impossible 7* will be in theaters, and I won't have to change a thing.

CONTINUED!

All I've changed is window dressing. Costumes. Music. Theme. Look. But the effect is priceless: an immediate image overhaul that gives this lesson a current cutting-edge feel, without touching a bit of the content.

Mission Accomplished.

Maybe moving without telling weird cousin Otto might be the best way to put a crimp in his regular visits. But, no matter what you do, Sunday is probably going to keep rolling around. Working several weeks ahead of the curve can keep things running like clockwork. And as you do, keep Learning Styles, The Rule of Three, The Application Factor, and The Style Makeover at the forefront of your planning process. These principles can help you make sure that your lessons are pre-loaded with power right from the start.

Sounds like a plan. And just in time. Because, don't look now ... Sunday's coming.

Talk, talk, talk, talk, **TALK**.

Man, I love to talk, don't you? I just can't get enough of the sound of my own voice. Especially when I think I'm being astoundingly brilliant and imparting others with the benefit of my vast wisdom and knowledge and expertise. I'll just go on and on and on and on, convinced I'm doing the world a service by blathering away, imparting information to the masses and ...

Shoot. I was doing it again, wasn't I? Sorry.

Seriously, as grown ups, we loooove to talk. Especially in Sunday school. Yes, yes, it's innocent and well intentioned enough. We imagine somewhere deep inside that if we just keep talking, some of it is bound to stick. If we just fill kids' heads with enough information, we'll make an impact.

But stop being an adult ... for just a minute ... and think back to the last truly memorable, unforgettable moment you experienced.

Really ... take a second and think it through.

No, don't just ignore me and keep reading. C'mon ... think back to a recent powerful moment in your life.

Okay, fine. Since you're determined to just keep on going, I'll give you a couple examples. Maybe it was witnessing the game-winning homerun live at a stadium that sent adrenaline coursing through your veins at mach 12. Perhaps it was an unbelievable special effect in a movie that had you gasping for breath. Or maybe it was even an intimate conversation that left you emotionally bonded with a friend or spouse. Chances are that the power of your last unforgettable moment,

84

whatever it was, involved very little talk. It probably wasn't about *information*. More than likely, it was some type of powerful *experience* that left an unshakable imprint on you. Am I right?

In fact, let's stretch this exercise even further, shall we? Think back to the gospels. Sure, Jesus did his fair share of talking. He could talk with the best of them—okay, better. But consider how much he valued the idea of experiential learning. He didn't just occasionally couple his words with unforgettable experiences for his listeners, he did it all the time!

Healings, miracles, storytelling, you name it—Jesus was all about creating unforgettable experiences to imbed truth into the hearts of his listeners.

A key difference between traditional teaching methods and creative teaching is the presence of powerful and unforgettable moments. It's not enough for me to just tell kids about the stories in the Bible—I want kids to experience them! (And let's get selfish for a sec ... as a teacher, I'm not content to just *talk* about this exciting stuff either; I want to live it! Experience it! Bring it to life! I know, it's all about me ...)

Sure, I can *tell* you the story of Jesus calming the storm. No problem. But what if I create a storm ... let you see it happen, right before your eyes? The loud pounding of the wind and thunder ... the wild fear in the disciples' eyes ... the awe of everything coming to a silent halt as Jesus simply utters, "Peace ... be still."

Which experience would you remember? Hearing about it? Or living it?

It's not enough to just tell Bible stories to kids. If we want kids to remember what we teach and be compelled and transformed by it, we must *bring* powerful Bible *moments to life*. We must help kids *experience* the Bible.

Just by using creativity, the arts, and some new methods (like the stuff included later in Part 3), you find that your teaching is becoming less about talking and much more about creating memorable, life-changing experiences. That's what we're after ...

LESS
YAPP-ENING

and

MORE
HAPPENING.

But using a new bag of tricks is only half the journey. By deepening your teaching *techniques,* you will create ever more powerful and unforgettable moments of Bible teaching.

There I go again ... falling in love with the sound of my own ... pen. Enough talk. Let's get down to the nitty-gritty and take a look at five specific techniques that can make your teaching—and the Bible—even more unforgettable.

STEP INTO THE STORY

When storytelling, we often narrate from outside the story. We *tell* what happened:

> "And then Jesse *told* David to go to the battlefield and take his brothers something to eat ... "

> "And then Jesus *told* the paralytic man to get up, take his mat and go home ... "

This form of narrative storytelling keeps you away from the heart of the story by making you an outside observer reporting the facts of the case. It also distances your audience from the potential emotion and power in the story. All it takes is a small adjustment to fine-tune your storytelling technique so it creates immediacy, intimacy, and a deep connection between the story and the audience. You simply need to step into the story.

Rather than talking about the characters, *become* the characters. Not necessarily all of them (though that's fun too). Pick moments to slip *into* the characters, giving your audience an immediate sense of being in the moment—a sense of witnessing this amazing happening right in front of them.

Let's consider this using a specific example. Instead of just reporting what Jesse said to David, *become* Jesse. Instead of telling *about* Goliath, *become* Goliath. Here's how it might play out:

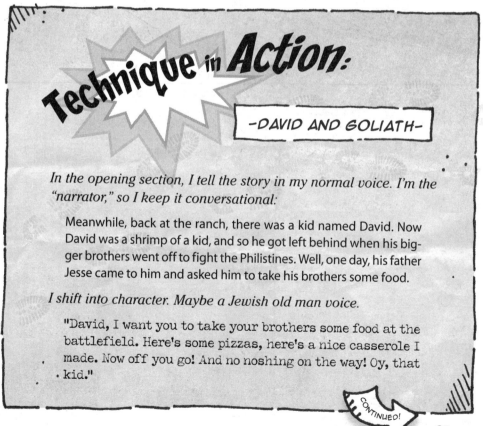

Technique in Action:

—DAVID AND GOLIATH—

In the opening section, I tell the story in my normal voice. I'm the "narrator," so I keep it conversational:

Meanwhile, back at the ranch, there was a kid named David. Now David was a shrimp of a kid, and so he got left behind when his bigger brothers went off to fight the Philistines. Well, one day, his father Jesse came to him and asked him to take his brothers some food.

I shift into character. Maybe a Jewish old man voice.

"David, I want you to take your brothers some food at the battlefield. Here's some pizzas, here's a nice casserole I made. Now off you go! And no noshing on the way! Oy, that kid."

CONTINUED!

I'm me again. Back to normal. It's seamless. As if nothing ever happened.

And so David headed out to the battlefield, but as he arrived, he heard Goliath, who had come out that day to issue his challenge to the Israelites.

My warrior voice kicks in. Booming. Rattling the room.

ISRAELITES!!!

For 40 days I have come out here
to challenge you,
and still, no one will face me!
You are a bunch of **sissies!!!**
On this day, I **curse** you,
I **curse** your army,
and I **curse** . . . . . .
your . . . . .
God!!!

I give it a second to settle over the room. Then I'm me again.

When David heard this, he couldn't believe his ears.

And so on. It's a simple and seamless transition. I don't have to physically refer to myself or say "I'm Jesse now" or anything goofy like that. The kids get it and track right along. They are immediately drawn into the storytelling as the moments unfold before their eyes. I could just report the facts, just the information, but *becoming* the characters heightens the humor and intensity and brings the story to life.

This technique can bring more poignant moments to life too. When I tell the story of Jesus and the Paralytic, I step into the role of Jesus to do just that. I often pull another adult volunteer out of the audience right before I tell the story (see Audience Participation in Part 3) to play the part of the "paralyzed man." I ask him to lie on the ground. My only quick and whispered instructions are, "Just follow my lead."

If I stayed outside the story as the narrator, he'd lay there like a lump the whole time. But I want the kids to *see* Jesus in this story. I want them to experience, to some small degree, the power of Jesus *connecting* with this real man who was forever changed by Jesus. By *becoming* Jesus, rather than just talking about him, the moment comes to life.

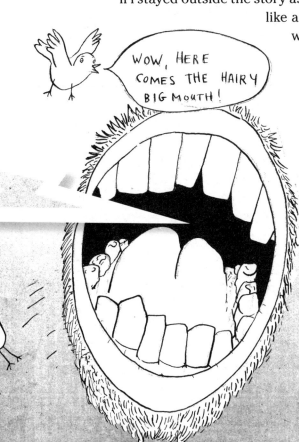

Technique in Action:

-JESUS AND THE PARALYTIC-

Hi. It's just me. Normal voice. I'm the narrator again.

When the hole was big enough, the men lowered their friend on a mat right down in front of Jesus. And the people were amazed! I mean, this was the man who, moments before, hadn't even been able to get near Jesus. Now he was right in front of him!

The moment is here: I become Jesus. I walk toward the paralyzed man. I kneel down to his level and look him in the eyes. I connect with him.

Softly. Gently.

Jesus said to the man ... "Get up."'

Wait ... wait ... wait.

"Take your mat and go home."

I don't look back at the audience because, as soon as I do, the connection will be broken. I watch the paralytic. I look into his eyes.

Awe-filled. Soft.

And the man ... sat ... up.

The volunteer slowly does. Every time.

All of a sudden, his arms could move ...

The volunteer does it. Every time.

His legs could move ...

Yep.

CONTINUED!

The man stood up ...

I wait for him to start to stand and I slowly rise with him. I haven't once taken my eyes away from his.

... picked up his mat ...

He'll do it.

... and walked right ... out ... through the crowd ...

Trust me, he will.

I watch him go—all the way back. I resist the urge to snap back into narration mode. I honor the moment and stay connected to this paralytic, even if he's all the way in the back of the room by now. And then ... rather than the more obvious choice to be energetic here ... I whisper ...

And the people were ... *amazed.* They praised God and said, "We have never seen anything like this before."

The technique of stepping into the role of Jesus never fails to illicit awe-filled silence and a sincere wow-factor from every audience of kids I've ever taught it to. If I stay *outside* the story, as a narrative story-teller, even if I say exactly the same script word-for-word, it never has that effect. But as soon as I *become* Jesus and make a *connection* with the paralyzed man, the power and wonder of the moment is real and present. We see Jesus respond to this guy as he begins to stand for the first time in his life. *That's* telling the story from the inside!

A Note About Gender ...

If you're a woman, you may be thinking, "Well, I can't *become* a man." And, if you're a man, perhaps teaching something like the story of the

Woman at the Well might cause you to think, "Well, I can't *become* a woman." Wrong. You can use this technique with great power regardless of gender. I have seen female teachers tell the story of Jesus and the Paralytic with awe and wonder by stepping into the part of Jesus. Obviously, they weren't men. Obviously, *you're* not Jesus. (If you think you are Jesus, then you have issues this book isn't prepared to address.) This isn't about literally becoming Jesus, of course. It is about bringing the moment to life. Gifted men and women can master this technique and *become* Jesse, Goliath, the woman at the well, and yes, even Jesus, and the kids won't bat an eye. They aren't looking to debate gender roles. They won't be thinking, "But you're a girl!" They'll be too wrapped up in the story to even notice one way or the other. And for once, that's just the way you'll want it.

USE THE POWER OF CONTRAST

A quick, hard gear-change. It's not so great during rush hour traffic. But during a lesson? Dynamite!

A sudden and unexpected shift in the tone or pacing of your lesson has the power to not only create a dynamic moment but also to draw attention to a main point or an especially compelling bit of application.

The lesson is uproariously funny. Then suddenly, you turn it serious and pointed ... that's contrast.

You're moving the lesson forward quickly, with energy and momentum. Then suddenly, you hit the brakes and emphasize a single sentence or thought ... that's contrast.

goliath, he was all mouth.

Sharp and unexpected tone shifts work great for moving from funny or energetic parts of the lesson, to more serious and direct points. By putting them right up against each other, you draw attention to the serious moment and it pops out.

grrrr

Let's take a look at this technique by going back to the story of David and Goliath.

Technique in Action:

—DAVID AND GOLIATH—

In this audience participation lesson, I've got a kid up front playing David. Another is dressed up like Goliath, standing on a chair. He has a big helmet on his head and a mop in his hands instead of a spear. Funny stuff. The lesson has been full of humor and silliness, with lots of energy and excitement up until this point. I want that momentum to continue all the way up until I turn on a dime toward the application.

My tone is energized. Fun. Light.

> But David looked at Goliath and said, "You may come at me with sword and ... **mop** ..."

Laughs from the kids. Good. They're enjoying themselves. Because I'm about to turn the corner. Hard.

> "... but I come at you in the name of the Lord God Almighty!"

> And so David took one of his stones and put it in his sling and slowly began to twirl it.

I grab David's hand and twirl it, making my own sound effects along the way. It's like a bad action movie. All part of the humor and the fun. The kids are roaring.

CONTINUED!

I twirl slowly at first, but then pick up speed.

whup
whup
whup
whup
whup
whup whup whup whup whup whup

David released the stone and the stone flew through the air and ...

Clap!

... smacked Goliath right in the middle of the forehead. And believe it or not, Goliath fell over.

I exaggerate moving out of the way, so as not to get crushed by Goliath. At this unspoken cue, the kid playing Goliath always falls over in a dramatic death scene—tongue hanging out, the whole bit.

... and died!

The group goes ga-ga. I'm talking over the roar of the crowd.

David had defeated Goliath using only a sling and a stone because God was on his side!

Thunderous applause! They're cheering David's victory. They're cheering Goliath's hammed up death scene. And then it happens. I slowly walk away from Goliath. My tone and demeanor shift immediately. Quiet. Pointed. Stark contrast from a moment ago. The response starts to die down. I wait it out.

Now.

I'm soft. Quiet. They have to lean in to listen. All ears are straining to hear me. Straining.

You probably won't run into any nine-foot giants when you go to school tomorrow. But you may have to face a giant problem.

Maybe you have to walk down to the bus stop for the first time by yourself, and that can be a scary thing.

Soft. Slow. Methodical.

Or maybe there's a kid at school who beats up on you … and you wake up every morning with a pit in your stomach because you know that he's there waiting for you.

Wait for it. Wait.

Or maybe…

HEY… ARE WE ALLOWED TO SAY THAT WORD IN CHURCH?

Wait for it.

maybe your parents are getting a divorce …

… and you feel like your whole life is falling apart …

… and you just don't know what you will do.

I look 'em right in the eyes. This is hardcore stuff and we all know it. My face is resolute. Strong. Fiercely compassionate. God is in the room. He always shows up for this.

SMACK ON THE KISSER!

You need to know this …

… the same God who stood on that battlefield with David …

… STANDS WITH YOU.

So you DO NOT NEED TO BE AFRAID.

And THAT is the story of David … and Goliath."

95

There is power in the room. Every kid is soaking up the awesomeness of God. The undeniable truth that God will be with them against giants and giant problems alike. The sharp contrast makes the application stand out and get noticed, which makes it all the more powerful and memorable.

What!? We're talking about divorce all of a sudden? We were just laughing it up. Kind of a downer, don't you think?

No way. The sharp contrast between the humor of the story and the intensity of the application smacks the kids right between the eyes. I

Figure 24.2e
One of many examples of
contrast found in the wild

can hear a pin drop when I say the word "divorce." The application is real and straight from their lives. When that kind of candor comes out of nowhere, it sucks them right in.

Maybe to you it would feel more natural to release your would-be David and Goliath back to their seats before diving into the more serious application. Natural instinct. Makes sense. But as soon as I release those kids back to the audience, the whole room momentarily unravels. The moment will pass and be lost forever. I've got them right where I want them. That's the time to turn on a dime and drive it on home.

A quick comment about age-appropriateness. I usually reserve something this bold and pointed for second grade and up. Not that you can't get serious with younger kids ... you can. But just be sensitive on how hard-hitting to get with issues like divorce, for example. Second grade and up, an issue like this is right where they're at.

USE THE POWER OF SILENCE

I find that we often feel apologetic about standing in front of kids if we're not talking every second. And yet, silence has amazing ability to bring everything to a halt. To give emphasis to a point.

SHHHH !

See what I mean? Got your attention, right? That's what intentional and unapologetic silence does in the midst of a teaching lesson.

The trick is to avoid overusing silence. Never use silence more than a couple times in any 25-minute teaching lesson. Used sparingly, silence gives weight and impact to meaningful or important points, poignant moments, or weighty content. Used willy-nilly, it can bog down a lesson and be the creative teaching equivalent of a tranquilizer dart in the rump.

You've already seen silence in action a little bit. Those "wait for it" moments in the David and Goliath story above were really little moments of silence. Now let's take a more focused look at this silent-but-deadly technique.

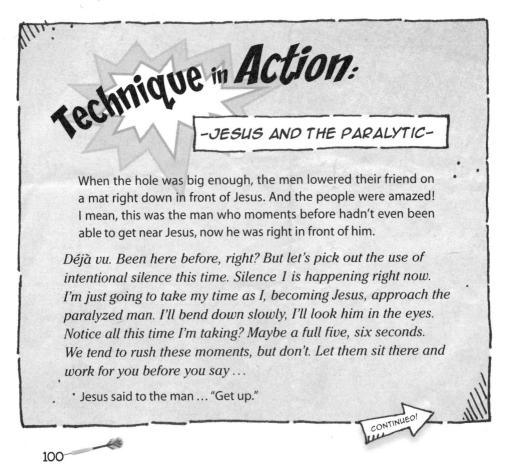

Technique in Action:

—JESUS AND THE PARALYTIC—

When the hole was big enough, the men lowered their friend on a mat right down in front of Jesus. And the people were amazed! I mean, this was the man who moments before hadn't even been able to get near Jesus, now he was right in front of him.

Déjà vu. Been here before, right? But let's pick out the use of intentional silence this time. Silence 1 is happening right now. I'm just going to take my time as I, becoming Jesus, approach the paralyzed man. I'll bend down slowly, I'll look him in the eyes. Notice all this time I'm taking? Maybe a full five, six seconds. We tend to rush these moments, but don't. Let them sit there and work for you before you say . . .

• Jesus said to the man . . . "Get up."

CONTINUED!

Wait. Just a moment or two. Not a full blown silence, just a baby one. A micro-silence. A semi-silence. Don't blast through this.

"Take your mat and go home."

And the man … sat … up.

I'm taking my time in this section.

All of a sudden, his arms could move …

Letting the moment linger.

His legs could move …

That doesn't mean lethargic.

The man stood up … picked up his mat … and walked right … out … through the crowd.

More like energized anticipation.

But now, as he walks out, I bring a the whole lesson to a stop. The moment hangs in midair as I watch the man walk out. Five. Six. Seven seconds. Feel it out. It often inadvertently brings me to tears—and it kinda should. It's a pretty amazing moment we're recreating here.

After letting the power of the moment sit, I return back to the kids, softly, honoring the silent connection that just happened in the story between Jesus and this man, the miracle that has taken place.

And the people were … *amazed.* They praised God and said, "We have never seen anything like this before."

If you feel like you always need to be running at the lips to deserve the kids attention, don't. True, you have to earn the right to use silence. But do that by keeping the rest of the lesson moving forward. Having done that, you have permission to bring everything to a screeching halt and let the moment sit. This silence emphasizes the miracle that just occurred. It underscores Jesus' power and authority. But more than that, it hammers home the connection between Jesus and this man—that, more than anything else, Jesus was all about people.

HANDLE THE BIBLE

Do I always read the story straight out of the Bible itself?

Nope. Almost never.

Okay, don't burn me as a heretic just yet. Put down the torches and pitchforks and I'll explain.

I (or the curriculum I'm using) typically rewrite the Bible story into kid language. That's part of being *intentional*. My job is not just to get the words out there; I need the words to be understood by my audience: kids.

But … there must be no doubt in kids' minds that the stories I'm teaching came from the Bible. How do I communicate that? Several ways.

I make sure that Bible verses are not only heard but seen. I usually put them on the screen with PowerPoint, and I always make sure that the specific reference is listed. When storytelling, I say that "in the Bible" it tells us about these things. I often slip this in several times throughout a lesson. But a supremely simple yet effective way to let them know that the story comes from the Bible is simply to hold it as I tell the story.

Am I reading it? No.

Is this license to blow off my memorization work and tape my teaching script into the Bible? No.

Am I saying that I should read it verbatim out of the Bible? Usually, no.

But by simply holding it open while I story tell (I don't even have to ever look at it), I give a clear and undeniable visual message: This story came from this book.

Do I want them to know that? No doubt.

CONTEMPORIZE THE MOMENT

I love the idea of making a Bible story accessible to kids, helping them to see themselves in the characters. Reality check: More often than we'd like to admit, kids tune out when the Bible story starts. We sometimes train them like Pavlov's dog to figure that the Bible part of the lesson is the boring part of the lesson. We say, "Today we've got a great Bible story for you ...," and then it winds up being a big snore-bore. Or worse, totally irrelevant.

Help kids see that these stories aren't just about a bunch of dead dudes. These stories are about *them.*

A pain-free way to get a little blip on the attention-o-meter is to look for strategic places you can contemporize the language. In other words, add some modern lingo, even pop culture references, to tug them in.

* FOR A PICTURE OF PAVLOV'S DROOLING DOG SEE PAGE 152.

Technique in Action:

-DAVID AND GOLIATH-

When Jesse sends David to the battlefield with the food.

> "David, I want you to take your brothers some food at the battlefield. Here's some pizzas, here's a nice casserole I made, now off you go! And no noshing on the way! Oy, that kid."

What food does the Bible say that David actually took? It doesn't. Like it matters. It could be Power Bars and Slim Fast for all I care. It's an easy little way to pop in a contemporization of the story. The kids always chuckle, and it pulls them just a notch or two deeper into the moment.

EXTRA ONIONS!

Phil's Pizza

SISSIE

CONTINUED!

How about when Goliath comes out on day 40 of his challenge to those wimpy Israelites?

ISRAELITES!!!

For 40 days I have come out here to challenge you, and still, no one will face me!

You are a bunch of **sissies!!!**

On this day, I curse you,

I curse your army,

and I curse ... your ... God!

Does the Bible say that Goliath called them a bunch of sissies? No. First Samuel 17:23 says that as David approached the battlefield, Goliath "shouted his usual defiance." Sounds like he was doing some trash-talkin' to me. Actually, he probably said something much cruder than sissies, but I'm not comfortable saying "wusses" in a lesson.

Just in a book.

you've still got BAD BREATH

Now, I'm not saying play fast-and-loose with the Bible. I'm not saying to colloquialize Jesus into a surfer dude or serve nachos and root beer at the Last Supper. Obviously, I don't want to cross a line and step on moments in which reverence needs to be honored. But, truth is, there are lots of little details in many stories that either aren't spelled out in the Bible or that don't really matter.

It doesn't matter what food Jesse gave David. The point is, he sent him to the battlefield. It doesn't matter exactly what Goliath called the Israelites. The point is, he was busting their chops. These are easy places to drop in some vernacular. Easy places to contemporize the language and make it something kids will relate to.

They know what it feels like to be called a sissy. And suddenly— *yank!*—they're pulled deeper into the story, deeper into that moment. And guess what? The "sissy" moment leads to "David's victory" moment.

And "David's victory" moment leads to the "God-is-with-you-even-if-you-parents-are-getting-a-divorce" moment.

And that may be the moment
that changes
everything
for one kid.

That's what moments do. That's the power of a moment.

DON'T BE ALARMED, XAVIER, BUT THERE'S A RATHER LARGE FROG ON THE NEXT PAGE.

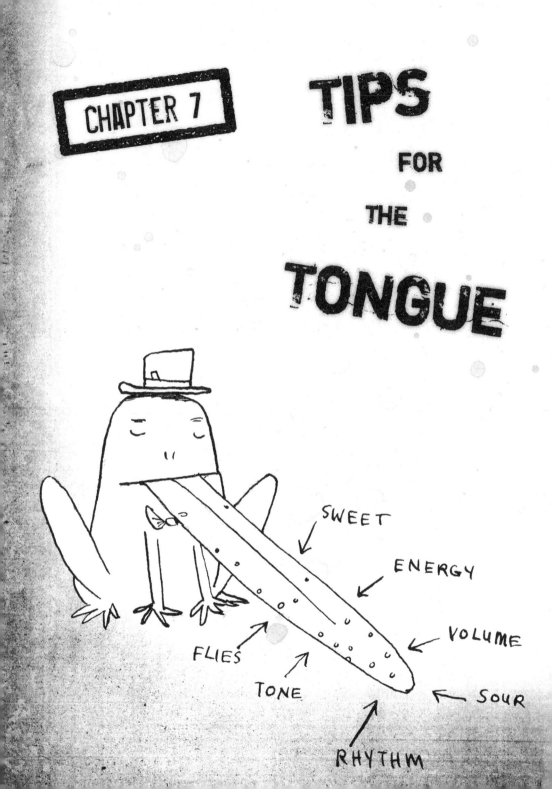

NOW HEAR THIS!!!

Sorry to shout. I just wanted to grab your attention, so I could share a little reminder about you and that voice box of yours: Your voice is a powerful tool. It has a dramatic power to shape the way kids perceive the material you're communicating.

108!!!!!!!!!!

Every couple years, in the days leading up to Holy Week, the "made-for-TV" people (whoever they are) release another Jesus movie. And I've picked up a common thread when it comes to these Bible-based miniseries events. Jesus always speaks with a British accent.

What's that all about?

Maybe the made-for-TV moviemakers think this elevates the content. Don't get me wrong; I love a lilting British dialect as much as the next guy. But this heightened treatment tends to make the material seem distant to me. Detached. Fine for watching the week before Easter but disconnected from the rest of my year.

But what if we changed the voice? Try something for me—a little imagination exercise, just for grins. Take a portion of Scripture, perhaps something Jesus said, and play it out in your mind ... audio only. Try this one:

> *"A new command I give you. Love one another. As I have loved you ... so you must love one another."*

Hear him say it. We probably all resort to that British dialect that we so often associate with Jesus ... the voice that comes with those miniseries movies and History Channel documentaries. But now, as this radio drama plays out in your mind, imagine the voice of Jesus changing. Recast Jesus, in your mind, with Robin Williams. Not the hopped-up, high-strung Genie-from-*Aladdin* version. Think Robin Williams from *Mrs. Doubtfire* when he's talking to Sally Field at the end. From *Hook*, when he's fallen back in love with his kids.

109

Just hear Jesus' words spoken in this new voice:

"A new command I give you. Love one another. As I have loved you ... so you must love one another."

A new Jesus takes shape, doesn't it? The realness of Robin's voice. The accessibility. The quickness he has for joy. You can almost hear his smile as he speaks, can't you?

It changes everything. Just by changing the voice.

When bringing the Bible to life for kids, your voice is one of the most powerful tools you have. Simple adjustments in pacing or energy, volume or rhythm, tone or inflection can change everything. They can enable you to build excitement. Create drama. Command attention. Diffuse a distraction.

Even shape the way a kid sees ... and hears ... Jesus.

DON'T TEACH, JUST TALK

Most of us would be mortified at the thought of talking down to our kids, and yet, we often do it without even realizing it. It's rooted in pure motives. We want kids to learn, to grab onto these biblical concepts that truly have the power to change their lives. We want to teach them. So we inadvertently adopt a teacher-y tone.

You know the one.

Voice somewhat higher than normal.

Lilting, sing-songy tone.

Enunciation of **words** exaggerated ever-so-**slight**ly.

Eyes **big**.

Eyebrows raised

Hello, boys and girls!

Even this word choice is a warning sign. Using "boys and girls" with any group older than first grade is a talking-down tip-off.

Exibit A: What "teaching" looks like

Today we are going to learn a wonderful Bible story about a man who learned that he could trust God no matter what.

Notice the rampant use of the word "learn" here? Subtle signal: *I'm here to TEACH you.*

It's important to identify these teacher-y tones with ruthless scrutiny. There's nothing wrong with wanting kids to learn. But when it comes to drawing them in, these subtle signals send the wrong message. If older kids feel talked down to, even if it's unintentional, they resent it. They disconnect. They unplug.

So don't teach. Just talk. If you sense that you may be afflicted by this down-talking syndrome, work on keeping your tone conversational. Authentic. Instead of trying to teach the kids, think of yourself as just hanging out with them. Casual conversational tones scream authenticity to kids, especially in second grade and up. This approachable "just talking" tone draws kids in and makes them feel respected. They recognize that you're relating to them on their own level, and they respond.

Hey, everybody! What's up?

When you speak, address them as friends. It's not the words themselves that are important here as much as the approachable tone they imply.

Man, I'm so glad you're here today, because I can't wait for you to hear this awesome story.

No hint of teaching. The tone is casual ... off-the-cuff ... immensely approachable. You authentically love this story and want to share it, like you'd share it with a friend.

Exibit B: What "teaching" sounds like

It's a story about incredible wars and vicious warriors. It's a story of mighty victories and horrible, bloody defeats.

You're luring them in. You're appealing to them on their level. It's engaging.

It's a story of courage. And faith. And trust in God.

No need to tell them who learned what. That sniffs of teaching. Give them the benefit of the doubt that they'll see what this Bible guy learned as they hear the story. You're just talking, just sharing something cool.

Casual.

Real.

Personal.

This tone draws kids in, rather than pushing them away.

So if you want to teach with power, don't teach. Just talk.

PEAKS AND VALLEYS

Most of us have a natural rhythm of speech. By rhythm, we're talking pacing, volume, and energy. This natural rhythm defines how we normally talk. Video yourself on the weekend sometime. You might be surprised by your natural teaching rhythm. You might find that you're a fast talker ... everything exits your mouth at breakneck speed. Or maybe your teaching rhythm tends to languish at a more sluggish pace. These natural rhythms may be fine in casual conversation with friends, but when charged with the responsibility of talking for 25 minutes, we owe our listeners vocal variety.

Think of your lesson like an amusement park ride. Carousel lessons go round and round at the same pace, energy, and speed. Fine for five minutes, but after 25 minutes even the most fanatical merry-go-round fan is ready to abandon horse for more exciting rides.

Wherever your natural speech rhythms fall on the teaching continuum, when you keep your rhythm at the exact same place during the whole lesson, you may be "vanilla-izing" the teaching. Lessons like this are hard to sit through. Important points are impossible to distinguish because everything sounds the same.

But exciting lessons are full of high peaks ... when energy moves forward, excitement and passion are present, humor is uproarious ... and loaded with low valleys ... when moments are soft and subtle, powerful poignancy is present, and God's holiness is highlighted through whispered awe.

Let's make our lessons roller-coaster rides. Full of unexpected swoops and swerves. Places where the pacing climbs slow and steady, and then careens uncontrollably forward with breakneck speed and excitement. The action-packed, emotionally charged Bible stories we teach aren't flat. They have peaks and valleys. So let your telling of these tales ride those ups and downs as well. You'll bring incredible power to your teaching.

Start with a little self-scrutiny. What is your natural rhythm? It may be hard to see for yourself. A video camera and an honest buddy could come in handy. Roll tape one weekend and watch it with a friend later, viewing ruthlessly to determine where your rhythm lives most of the time. Chances are, you'll find a common through-line to your rhythm.

As
    a
      slow
        talker,
          do

you
    tend
      to
        languish?

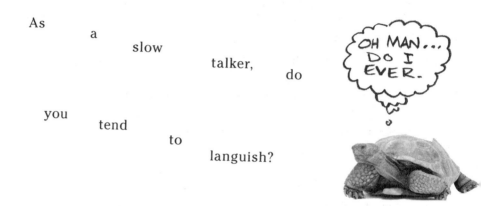

Then you may want to crank up your pacing a few notches to discover a slightly more energized natural rhythm across the board. Don't dwell on every sentence. That way, when you do dwell, it will stand out.

Are you a fast talker, speeding past poignant moments in an effort to race to the end? Then maybe back off the gas a bit, so when you kick your lesson into overdrive, it really stands out.

Making these subtle adjustments to your rhythm is an ongoing process, one that takes time. Your natural rhythm is habit. So is mine. But our ultimate goal is the ability to use any rhythm we choose to match the moment, rather than just maintaining a predetermined pace out of habit.

Once you've identified your natural rhythm, it's time to take a close look-see at your lesson and determine where the peaks and valleys belong, according to the story. Pick out the parts where the action drives forward ... peaks. ID the places where the moment is soft and poignant ... valleys. These ups and downs invigorate the storytelling.

Take a look....

Technique in Action:

-JESUS' LAST DAY-

This story is easy to whitewash with one tone. Because it deals with the crucifixion, it seems natural to tell the whole thing with a somber mood. But this is a story with ups and downs, and we need to bring the kids along on this roller-coaster ride.

This first part can be kept simple. Just talk.

> The leaders dragged Jesus to the governor, whose name was Pilate. But after questioning Jesus, Pilate couldn't find that he'd done anything wrong and wanted to let him go.
>
> But the Jewish leaders wouldn't put up with that.

Now it's starting to build. We're entering a peak here in the energy. Increasing the excitement. Upping the volume. Picking up the pacing.

> So they went out and got the crowds of people to shout, demanding that he be killed.

Peak! Yell it. Become the crowd.

> "Crucify him!" they shouted.

Into overdrive now ... keep moving the pacing forward toward the next peak ... you want the kids to feel the frenzy of the crowd ... the panic ... the force of the moment.

> And Pilate was worried that the crowds were going to go nuts and take over the place ... so even though he didn't think Jesus had done anything wrong ... he gave the orders to his guards.

CONTINUED!

Pant, pant, pant. There should be a rush from the intense drive of this section.

Now, full stop. The bottom drops out ... an abrupt and unexpected valley. This next moment needs weight ...

"Crucify him," he said.

Now we ease back off. If every moment is a high point or a low point, then none of them feel like one. Sometimes you just have to back off and talk. Like now. You don't need to play the mood here, the words are powerful enough.

So the guards took Jesus back to the prison. But before taking him out to nail him to the cross, they decided to have some fun with him.

Simple. Subtle. Not too moody or overly sad. Let the words do their job.

Fun for the guards, not Jesus. Jesus' Jewish followers had always called him "King of the Jews." Well, the guards thought it might be funny that this king was now a lowly prisoner who was sentenced to die.

Pick up the pace, slowly driving toward "What's wrong, King of the Jews?" A gradual build toward this new peak ...

So they made a phony crown for him, out of thorns, and they pushed this into his head until the thorns stabbed him and he bled. Then they put a purple robe on him and gathered around him and pretended to bow down and worship him. "What's wrong King of the Jews?"

Peak!!

If you teach a lesson like this with slow, languid pacing, it loses power. The whole thing gets spray-painted with one tone, and no individual moments pop out. By giving the story the highs and lows it deserves,

psssh

it becomes an experience, a journey rather than just information. Even a kid who knows the story in detail gets drawn into an experience like this.

Up. Down. Dips. Plunges. Thrills. Spills. The roller-coaster may leave you breathless, but I'll take it over the merry-go-round any day.

SOFTENING

No matter how great your kids are and no matter how masterful you are at bringing the Bible to life, kids will be kids. They get squirrelly. Squiggly. Chatty.

But the moment you stop your lesson to say "shhhh," two things happen.

First, you yank everyone out of any moment you were trying to create. The story of Moses parting the Red Sea gets immediately washed away as you try to separate Travis and Jack from their whispered conversation about their newest Bionicles. The hushed awe of Jesus calming the storm gets upstaged by you hushing that cluster of girls comparing Neopets in the back of the room.

Second, you give the kids the power. Kids revel in it when they know they have the ability to throw grown-ups off their game. There's no better signal to the kids that they are in control than allowing them to bring your well-prepped lesson to a grinding halt.

Sometimes, we try another tack. Instead of stopping the lesson to dole out shooshes, we put the "drown-them-out" method into play. We think if we just talk a little louder, we'll send a subtle signal that they're being rude and we'll make ourselves heard over the whispered hubbub. But anyone who has tried this drown-them-out defense has probably observed the inevitable: the kids talk louder themselves, as if the timbre of your voice was just a loud air conditioner that needed to be compensated for.

Nope, talking louder doesn't do the job.

So how do you squelch these chatty distractions, when kids get fidgety?

BRUNHILDA IS EXPOSED TO THE CONCEPT OF SOFTENING.

Here's an incredibly effective technique for quashing a case of the chatties: softening.

You're in the middle of your lesson about Saul on the road to Damascus. You're approaching the moment when Jesus appears to Saul and blinds him. But regrettably, the group of fifth-grade boys in the back has chosen this moment to become engrossed in making rude mouth noises.

The last thing you want to do is give them the spotlight. You want to lure them back in, along with every other kid, without acknowledging the distraction in the first place. So you soften. Volume dips. Intensity increases. Rather than making this moment of Jesus appearing to Saul into a big brouhaha, bring it to a soft and poignant place. Play into the quiet power of the story, and watch the yakking bite the dust as kids refocus.

Here's a snapshot of it in action:

Technique in Action:

-THE ROAD TO DAMASCUS-

You're in the middle of your lesson. Everything is going great ...

As the message about Jesus spread, so did opposition. People began actually hunting down Christians to stop them from spreading the message. One of the most effective Christian-hunters was a guy named Saul.

Saul was absolutely convinced that this message about Jesus ... was wrong. He was committed to stopping it from spreading, even if he had to kill every follower of Jesus.

Uh oh. You can hear the titter starting. Those boys in the back are starting to unravel a little.

But Saul was changed forever when Jesus appeared to him on the road to Damascus. A bright light shined in the middle of his path, and a voice ...

Now they're doing their mouth-noises ... they don't mean to be rude, but they've become distracted, and they're goofing around now. It's time to draw them back in, before they become the focus of the room. And it's right at the most important moment of your story too. Isn't that always the way?

Sink to your knees here, maybe. Don't make a big dramatic deal of it, trying to shock them back into attention. Become Saul ... but begin to soften ... use the awe of the moment ...

... a voice of power ... spoke to him.

Stay on your knees ... wait ... use a moment of silence. That will speak to those boys. Even if they are still talking ... the fact that

CONTINUED!

119

they are the only ones talking, but they haven't thrown you … well, that's a very powerful message.

Then … softly … slowly …

"Saul, why do you hurt me like this?"

You hadn't planned on getting soft here, but you're responding to the boys, using this softening technique in the moment. Their attention should have started to perk up after that moment of silence and softness. But be prepared to sustain it as long as you need to pull them back into the game.

Saul didn't understand who this could be.

"What?" he said. "Who are you?"

Again … soft. Underplayed. Let Jesus' power emanate with soft intensity. You still haven't acknowledged the boys and their shenanigans …

"I am Jesus. The one you are persecuting. Well, get up and go into the city. I've got plans for you."

Did I just use the word shenanigans? Sorry about that …

Sustain another moment of silence … let the authority of the moment do its work. You've got them! They're back with you, and you never had to give them the keys to the car. You stayed in control …

Now's the time to ease back to your normal volume and pace. The point has been made … NOTHING is going to rob this story of its power. Nothing is going to stop it from being told.

When he got up from the ground and opened his eyes, he found that he couldn't see anything.

But he made his way to the town of Damascus, where a man named Ananias found him.

And on the lesson goes …

This softening technique takes some practice. It requires solid prep-aration (that is, memorization), so you can be fully engaged in the moment and ready to adjust the dynamic of the lesson to unexpected moments of distraction, rather than be thrown by them. But the power is palpable.

Trying to out-talk those boys would never have gotten the job done. By dropping the volume out of the lesson and replacing it with whispered intensity, the little mouth-fart contest in the back becomes the loudest thing in the room, which immediately makes those boys incredibly self-aware. Their ears perk up. Their attention redirects. They sense the silence and wonder … they realize they're missing something. And in that moment … you've got them. You've re-directed their attention, and sent a very clear message to every kid in the joint:

> *I'm in the driver's seat.*
>
> *I have an unbelievable story to tell.*
>
> *A journey to take you on.*
>
> *And it will not be run into the ditch by silliness.*
>
> *I will not be derailed.*
>
> *So buckle up and don't miss it.*

The way you use your voice can alter everything. And while the made-for-TV people are unlikely to change their approach and cast Robin Williams as Jesus (bummer), you and I can change the way we use our voices for dramatic results. Changes in volume, rhythm, inflection, and pacing ... these adjustments can alienate kids or draw them to you. They can flatten a lesson or make it a roller-coaster ride of peaks and valleys. They can diffuse a distraction, without saying a disciplinary word.

So much power ... right on the tip of your tongue.

CHAPTER 8

MASTERING MOVEMENT

Little known fact: I graduated from college with a minor in dance.

Get your giggles out … it's true. I spent hours pirouetting and ponte-chetting in ballet class. I fox-trotted and polka-ed my way through ballroom dance. I logged loads of time filapping and shuffle-ball-changing in tap class.

Great, you say. *Now I have to tap-dance to keep my kids attention during the Bible lesson?*

Not unless you want to.

Since I began refocusing my creative abilities onto the fabulous world of children's ministry, opportunities to put my fancy footwork to good use have been few and far between. But my schooling in the nimble-footed arts has left me keenly aware of one thing. Your voice isn't the only piece of equipment God gave you in preparation for powerful teaching.

When it comes to facing down a roomful of kids, I often hear frustrated teachers complain that they simply don't know what to do with their bodies.

The result? Lessons filled with aimless wandering and empty gestures that rob their words of strength and punch.

But that bod of yours is a powerful tool in the quest for dynamic Bible teaching. How you use movement during your lessons can communicate worlds beyond the words you speak. By mastering a few simple movement techniques, you can position yourself for power, stress and underscore your points, and create variety and excitement.

It's time to get moving! Jump in and tackle these techniques and take your lessons from languid to truly moving. No tap dancing or tutus required.

DIAGNOSING DRIFT

When in doubt, just move around a lot. When faced with a potentially excruciating 20 minutes of standing in front of kids without any ideas about what to do with your body, you may sometimes revert to this walkabout philosophy.

But this move-around-a-lot idea leads to a common movement malady: drift. There's nothing worse than a bad case of drift. Fortunately, there's an ointment that takes away the itch.

Okay, enough of the bad medical humor. Drift is a code name for aimlessly wandering throughout a lesson. When we aren't sure what to do with our bodies, we just drift. When we catch well-intentioned tips that we should "just move around a lot" but aren't equipped to make the movement count, we drift.

So ... I need to ask you a rather personal question: Are you suffering from drift? Side effects may include aimless wandering around during lessons, shifting your weight uncomfortably from one foot to the other, shuffling of feet, and empty throwaway arm gestures.

Far from infusing a lesson with variety or interest, all that shuffling and shifting actually diffuses the energy from a lesson and robs it of power. Fortunately, drift is completely curable. Like so many things, knowing is half the battle.

So how do you self-check for drift? Well, if you're not sure what to do with yourself during lessons, this could be a tip-off that you struggle with drift. As with other things, a video camera or an evaluation buddy can confirm the diagnosis. Once you identify the telltale roaming and shuffling for what it is, the solution is simple:

Cut it out!

Okay, simply said, but not simply done. Here's a three-step program to dealing with drift and getting some power-packed movement back into your step.

STEP 1

Anchor Yourself

Plant yourself in one spot—both feet on the ground, weight evenly distributed. And don't move. Don't shuffle. Don't even wiggle your baby toe. Now try to deliver a portion of your lesson. It's a whole new ball game. Welcome to anchoring.

A great first step for those struggling with drift, I highly suggest anchoring yourself in this way for a good bit of your lessons. At first, all you'll feel is stiff and uncomfortable. You'll say, "This can't be right! I'm just standing here!" You'll find yourself creeping away

AT FIRST I WAS STIFF AND UNCOMFORTABLE

NO PROBLEM WITH DRIFT →

126

or shifting weight out of habit. This is a natural reaction, as your body rebels to the enforced stillness and cries out to wander aimlessly around the teaching area as in days of old. Force yourself to stay anchored. The squirmy feelings will pass with practice.

As time goes on, you will feel the authority that anchoring gives. No longer diffused by aimless meandering, your lesson will take on a grounded, power-filled focus. Do not resist the sensation. This is anchoring doing it's work ... ridding you of the ambling that once diluted your energy and concentrating it into a strong and focused delivery.

Now, am I saying that you should remain stock-still like a statue for the remainder of your volunteer teaching tenure? Nuh uh. You don't want to just stand and talk from here to kingdom come. Don't get me wrong, strategic stillness like this is a very strong position, and I use it a lot to emphasize key points. Just standing anchored and delivering teaching with authority is *always* a more potent position than just drifting around. But early on, it's a great step away from drift toward more intentional, well-chosen movement. Think of it as an extreme movement makeover.

Put Your Hands in Your Pockets

Public speakers and speech-givers decry this as a major no-no, but don't listen to the lies. You can put your hand in your pockets.

You totally can.

I'm a big fan of hands in the pockets. Not all the time, but sometimes it's a great stance, especially if you struggle with drift. It's a very casual, approachable posture that really spells out relateability to kids. But it also has the bonus feature of anchoring you. It's really hard to wiggle and wander around with your hands crammed into your Levis. And since this pocket-stuffed approach presents a very casual attitude, it's also a great crutch to help you move toward "just talking" if you tend to adopt teacher-y tones, as we discussed in chapter 7.

STEP 2

Replace Drift with Intentional Movement

This is the ultimate goal. Make your movement count. When you move during a lesson, move for a reason.

Shift to short agitated movement when the story gets intense. Walk slowly and deliberately downstage to emphasize an important point. Stop and anchor yourself at pointed moments, but then casually roam (not to be confused with drifting) near the edge of the stage during more casual, off-the-cuff segments.

Let's take a run at intentional movement with an example:

PIRATE FOOTPRINT →

Technique in Action:

-JESUS IN THE GARDEN-

Set the stage, establish the mood. This is a story that takes place in a very specific location. You might start upstage center, and walk slowly down. Look around. Take it in. You're in the garden. You can establish that without ever saying so, just with movement.

A peaceful garden. Gethsemane. It was a place Jesus had gone to many times before with his disciples to pray. And it started out quiet on this night too.

Here's a major abrupt shift. Agitation! Anger! Loud! Torches! Clubs! Let your movement become what you're saying here! Walk around aggressively, change directions quickly, flail your arms on "clubs"...

But it wouldn't be long before it would be

LOUD,

full of **angry voices,**

and people holding

TORCHES AND CLUBS!

Now back to calm. Abrupt shifts in movement and physical pacing like this make the danger you just foreshadowed stand out.

CONTINUED!

But for now it was quiet.

Now this next section is backstory ... not quite as important as the rest. It's like when the announcer says

"Previously on Lost ..."

... a reminder of what happened just before this. So you might stroll over to the far right-hand side of your teaching space. By doing that, you establish two "spaces" ... a "garden" space in which you'll tell the story, and a "narrative commentary" space in which you'll just be you and bring the kids up to speed.

If you remember, Jesus left the Last Supper and took his disciples to this garden to pray. He knew that the time was almost here for him to die. And that was a hard thing to think about. He was a little worried. And he was probably scared.

When he came to the garden to pray to God, to get strength, he knew he had a choice. He could walk away and not go through with this. But he knew God's plan was the right one. If Jesus didn't do this, we would always be separated from God. He loved us too much to let that happen.

We're going back to the garden now, so physically go back to your center "garden" space. Re-enter the space again. See how we're moving with purpose? Every movement is intentional ... no drifting.

So he entered the garden of Gethsemane to pray. He asked most of his disciples to stay at the edge of the garden and rest, but he took three of them — Peter, John, and James — deeper into the garden to watch over him while he prayed. He knew even now that the betrayer was with the Jewish leaders, and they would soon be coming to get him, to take him away. But he needed strength from God to face what was coming.

CONTINUED!

Remember "stepping into the story" from chapter 6? Here it is. Kneel. Become Jesus, saying the prayer. But don't talk in a British accent (unless you're British). Just talk. Make it Jesus just talking to Dad. This simplicity models to kids that prayer isn't this elaborate ceremony, it's something they can do anytime, like breathing.

This was Jesus' prayer, "God, if there is another way to do your plan, without me having to die, please take this away from me."

Stay kneeling, but redirect your attention back to the kids for this little narration ...

But that wasn't the end. He then said...

Now eyes back to God. Pick a single point of focus and ... just ... talk.

"But your will be done, not mine. I want to do what you want , not what I want, because you know best."

Intentional movement. That's movement that adds to the lesson, strengthens it, partners with it.

Free from distraction.

Free from awkward uncertainty.

Free from drift.

SIT FOR STRESS

BIC.

Creative teaching aside, this little abbreviation has helped me immensely as a *writer*. Sometimes I don't feel like writing, but I need to write anyway. If I stand around waiting for inspiration to strike, I could be waiting a long time. The very act of sitting down and forcing my hands to the keyboard often finds inspiration meeting me there. So I believe firmly in BIC.

BIC? → **Butt In Chair.**

This little mantra is also a fabulous recipe for moments of poignancy, intimacy, or stress in a teaching lesson. All right, it doesn't have to be a chair your bottom sinks into. But just the intentional act

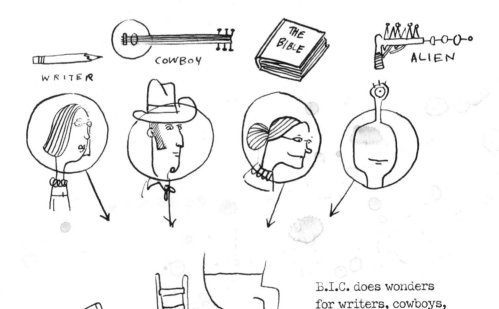

WRITER

COWBOY

THE BIBLE

ALIEN

B.I.C. does wonders for writers, cowboys, Sunday school teachers, and yes, from time to time, aliens.

Thank you for
not sitting on
the sea urchins
—Aquarium
management

of sitting at a specific moment in the lesson sets that moment apart and brings it into sharp focus.

Try starting a lesson sitting casually on a stool or in a gooshy chair. Most of us typically start our lessons on two feet, but a reclined posture sets a more approachable, casual tone right from the get-go. It says, "Hey, we're hanging out and talking," which translates into draw-me-in appeal with kids.

Starting a lesson from sitting also gives you somewhere to go. Think about a singer ... if she starts with all her fancy-schmancy trills and high notes right out of the gate, then she's shown her whole hand from the start and has nowhere to progress to. It's stronger for her to start simple and work her way toward the crescendo.

Same with you and your lesson. By simply sitting at the start, you give yourself new places to go in the lesson movement-wise ... at some point you'll need to stand ... and then move toward the kids ... and then move away from them ... and suddenly you have a journey to take them on rather than just doing the same stand-and-deliver routine the whole time. Sitting sometimes makes a nice start to the journey.

Picking a spot in the midst of the lesson to sit is also prime for creating softer moments of intimacy or vulnerability. A personal story screams for a good sit-down. Try the edge of the teaching stage or even the floor on for size.

In a lesson on forgiving your enemies, maybe you decide to share the story about how, in the seventh grade, Suzy Quidmeyer took your jeans from the gym locker room and hid them and you had to walk all the

YA YA, THINK ABOUT ME AND MY BEAUTIFUL FANCY-SCHMANCY TRILLS!

way to the nurse's office with nothing but a towel wrapped around your waist. Gasp! That's pretty exposed, in every sense of the word. But a personal story like this is a powerhouse for drawing kids in. They want to know all about the Suzy Quidmeyer fiasco and how you struggled to forgive her for this most unforgivable of acts. It puts skin on the bones of the biblical teaching. Intimacy and vulnerability are the order of the day. So have a seat. Cop a squat on the edge of your teaching stage—or even right on the floor at eye-level with the kids. This close contact and simple act of sitting gives weight and empha- sis to this moment. Completely unspoken, it tells the kids, "This is a personal moment for me. But I'm going to invite you into this exposed moment, because you are my friends." And the kids are all ears.

Picking a spot to sit in the lesson also helps to stress important points.

Here's how:

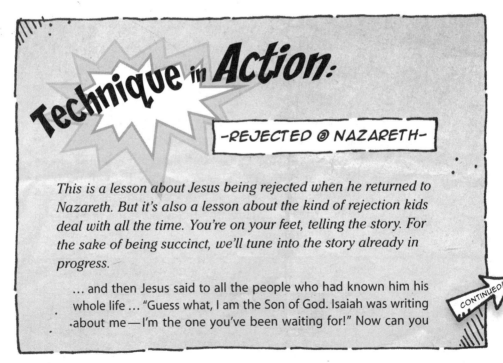

Technique in Action:

—REJECTED @ NAZARETH—

This is a lesson about Jesus being rejected when he returned to Nazareth. But it's also a lesson about the kind of rejection kids deal with all the time. You're on your feet, telling the story. For the sake of being succinct, we'll tune into the story already in progress.

... and then Jesus said to all the people who had known him his whole life ... "Guess what, I am the Son of God. Isaiah was writing about me—I'm the one you've been waiting for!" Now can you

CONTINUED!

imagine sitting in that room hearing someone you used to babysit for or play in the sandbox with, say "I am the Son of God." And the people were like, "This is Jesus, right? The carpenter's son?" They refused to believe him and they ended up getting so angry with him that they drove him out of town to the edge of the highest cliff and got ready to throw him off. That's how much they hated Jesus.

Remember anchoring? This is the place. It's the perfect spot to stand and deliver.

I'm sure Jesus felt rejected. Especially 'cause these were people who had known him his whole life, and now they were ready to kill him and throw him off a cliff! So in the face of teasing and rejection, what does Jesus do? Now remember he really was the Son of God, so he had the power to do anything he wanted. He could have had angels come down and fight; he could have performed a miracle to prove to everyone who he was; or he could have just had lightning strike them all. But what did Jesus do? The Bible says he walked right through the crowd and went on his way.

Movement should shift here ... you want to reach out to the kids with these words and your movement should reflect it. Act out the moment ... maybe jump up on a chair at the "Superhero" moment ...

Can you believe that? Is that what you would have done? I don't think I would have. I probably would have let them throw me off the cliff and then stopped midair and flown up above all of them Superhero style, and then said, "See ya!" and just kept on flying.

But Jesus didn't *say* or *do* anything. People said to him, "You're not the Son of God," and it didn't faze him, 'cause he knew the truth. He knew he was, so he was free to just walk away. Don't you want to be like that? I want to be like that. So then we've gotta flip the way we see ourselves.

Here comes the point to stress. Have a seat. Sit on the edge of the stage, or a stool, but sit. Lean forward, elbows on knees. This is your moment of emphasis. This is the point of the story.

Here's how: **KNOW WHAT'S TRUE**. People say mean things to us like "you're stupid" and it's easy to believe them; to think that what they're saying is *true*, but that's when we need to know what's *really* true; to know what Jesus says about us.

So alright, what is the truth? Who does Jesus say you are? He says you are a MASTERPIECE. That God made each and every one of us to be our own beautifully unique works of art—some with green eyes ...

And so on.

If you spend the whole teaching time on your feet, but then you choose to sit down at a key moment of important content, it makes that content sizzle a little more loudly. The point you made when you parked yourself will bubble to the top of the kids' retention.

Strategic sitting gives your lesson physical peaks and valleys to match the vocal ones you're creating.

It gives you a solid starting place.

It's a great way to get up close and personal during a story.

It stresses important points.

So when preparing a powerful lesson, don't be afraid to sit down on the job.

POSITION YOURSELF FOR STRENGTH

Whether you teach from an actual stage, a barely raised teaching platform, or just a square at the front of the room taped off with masking tape, there are some 101-level stage principals that can position your lessons for more movement-based power.

In theater, different areas of the stage have different names. Upstage. Downstage. Center stage. If your kids have ever been involved in high school productions or you've trod the stage yourself in days gone by, then these terms are probably familiar to you.

What may be new knowledge, however, is that different places on the stage carry different weight in terms of how much presence and power you have in your audience's eyes. And that's some knowledge worth putting a spotlight on. Because, regardless of your ministry size or teaching space, these stage directions can help you move your teaching to the strongest position possible.

ARE YOU TIRED OF BEING PUSHED AROUND AT THE BEACH?

EAT YOUR WHEATIES!

137

So here's a top ten list of stage direction details worth knowing.

TOP TEN FACTS FOR STRONG STAGE POSITIONING

1. Downstage ... that's the area closest to your audience.

2. Upstage ... that's further back, away from your audience.

3. Center stage ... you guessed it. Right in between.

4. These phrases come from the early days of Greek theater when the stage was actually raked, or tilted down toward the audience. Thus, downstage was literally ... down. That's a less practical detail and mostly for you history dorks out there.

5. Downstage is a position of strength. You're closer to your kids. Things you say from downstage have more presence ... more weight ... more strength. But not if you deliver *everything* from downstage. So when making main points, move downstage. It makes those main points pop.

6. Midstage or upstage is a great place to live and linger. It makes the times you deliberately walk downstage stand out as more unique and unexpected.

7. Putting your back to your audience is okay. Walking away from your audience is permissible ... regardless of what your high school drama director told you. In fact, it can be delicious in small doses, kind of like Thousand Island dressing.

I'll often walk upstage and away from the kids during a silence, to build drama or intrigue, before I launch into a more forward-driving section.

8. Asymmetry is appealing. So while your instincts may tell you to sit center stage during that Suzy Quidmeyer story, sitting center is also predictable. Sit downstage just right or left of center for a less symmetrical, more visually interesting position.

9. Create specific locales on stage, even if they're only in your head, like we did with the garden of Gethsemane a few pages back. When storytelling David and Goliath, there's no need to just stand in one spot or roam around aimlessly. Even if you don't have any actual characters to work with, position your imaginary Israelites on one side and your imaginary Philistines on the other. In your mind, put Goliath upstage and David down. This gives you a place to travel to during each section of the story and paints a visual picture for the kids as you move through your paces.

And **10.** These are guidelines, not absolutes. Sometimes you just have to feel it. So take some chances. Try some things. And use rehearsal the way God intended ... for figuring it out.

Don't be thrown by all the stage-speak. You don't have to be an accomplished actor or a dance diva to position yourself for strength. No matter how big your teaching space is, these principals can add dynamic strength to your teaching as you become familiar with how to use a variety of positions on the stage for different purposes.

LEVEL OUT

You're at the circus. You're watching the ringmaster.

"Ladies and gentlemen! Prepare yourself to be truly amazed!"

You know. That whole ringmaster drill.

"I present to you ..."

He's announcing the next act, but you don't see them anywhere. Then, suddenly...

"... the Flying Tabascos!"

The spotlight shines and your attention is immediately redirected ... upward! Of course! But you never saw it coming.

This is a wonderfully simple concept of using levels to create variety and unexpectedness. And while your Sunday school is certainly no circus (though evidence may at times point to the contrary ...), this is an easy technique we can use to create visual variety of the unexpected kind.

Think high. I've had great success with scaffolds, like a painter uses. I'll wheel one in as part of my teaching space decor, and during a video segment, I'll climb up there. When the lights go on, I teach sitting on the edge, three levels up. What a wonderful way to do the Sermon on the Mount. Or Moses on the mountaintop. Or the transfiguration. The effect is every bit as wonderful as looking skyward for the Flying Tabascos. The kids never see it coming, so they're immediately drawn in.

What about a ladder? Or some hay bales stacked three high? Any option that gives you some new vertical space to explore is an option worth climbing up and checking out.

Also think low. How about coming out of a manhole to

deliver a specific section of teaching? All right, so you're probably not going to cut a hole in your floor so Jonah can emerge from the hold of the boat. But if your teaching stage is built from sectional risers, then making a gap to create a down-under entrance could be a cakewalk.

I once saw a ministry that had the front half of a Volkswagen bug on their teaching stage, and they used the trunk (remember, the bug's trunk is on the front) as an entryway for the teachers. What about crawling out of a pup tent? How about hanging a clothesline on which to clip storytelling props ... but this time, position it really low so you teach laying on your back, limbo-style, as you pin up those props. Sounds twisted, I know, but I guarantee your kids will sit up and take notice.

So think vertically. A whole new dimension of movement possibilities will pop to the surface, leveling out your lessons with kid-friendly variety, interest, and excitement.

I'm sad to say I've never gotten to put my dance experience into practice in children's ministry. Well, unless you count that little jig I did during the Christmas musical a couple years back. But that was more of a hoppy-type thing.

And should Caesar Augustus really have to dance anyway? I think that's the real question.

Regardless ... now you won't have to two-step to keep your kids' attention either. With a few new movement skills tucked into your tights, you'll be teaching to a new groove in no time.

And your kids will be tapping right along.

blip... blip... blip... blip... blip... blip...

CHAPTER 9

RELEVANCE: KEEPING CURRENT

Wanna find out how well you know kids?
Well, pull out your number two pencil.
Keep your eyes on your own paper.
You know the drill.
Because the relevance quiz begins … *now*.

Name: Me

1. **Which of the following is *not* a real PS2 video game duo?**
   a. Ratchet & Clank   c. Jak & Daxter
   b. Mixter & Mondo   d. All of the above

2. **Which phrase is commonly used by SpongeBob SquarePants to express frustration?**
   a. Fish guts!   c. Tartar sauce!
   b. Musk melons!   d. Starfish!

3. **There are a lot of TV shows out there that deal with the occult. Which is *not* one of them?**
   a. *Charmed*   c. *So Weird*
   b. *Supernatural*   d. *A Black Cat Named Bob*

4. **Fourth and fifth graders are not experimenting with sex. True or False?**

5. **Which of the following is really a favorite snack among kids?**
   a. Froot-tastik   c. Fruit Gushers
   b. Fun by the Foot   d. Fruit Tape

144

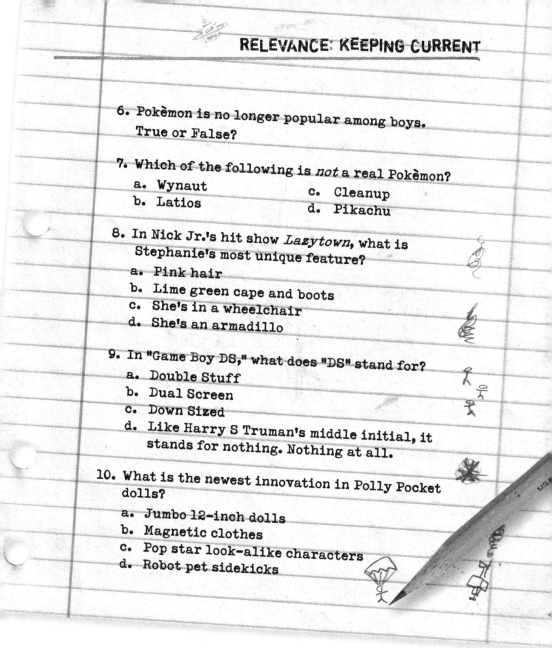

6. Pokèmon is no longer popular among boys. True or False?

7. Which of the following is *not* a real Pokèmon?
   a. Wynaut
   b. Latios
   c. Cleanup
   d. Pikachu

8. In Nick Jr.'s hit show *Lazytown*, what is Stephanie's most unique feature?
   a. Pink hair
   b. Lime green cape and boots
   c. She's in a wheelchair
   d. She's an armadillo

9. In "Game Boy DS," what does "DS" stand for?
   a. Double Stuff
   b. Dual Screen
   c. Down Sized
   d. Like Harry S Truman's middle initial, it stands for nothing. Nothing at all.

10. What is the newest innovation in Polly Pocket dolls?
    a. Jumbo 12-inch dolls
    b. Magnetic clothes
    c. Pop star look-alike characters
    d. Robot pet sidekicks

Okay, pass your papers to the front of your row ... oh, sorry. Grade school flashback.

Before we check our work, let's get a couple things straight. So if you're reading this even a couple years after I wrote it, the questions themselves may be already out of date, let alone the answers. And if you're reading this in 2050, O children's minister of the future, you're probably wondering (as you drive your flying car to your job at the cyborg plant): *What in the world is a Polly Pocket?*

This is the challenge we face … the current affairs in a kid's world change quickly. But, just for fun, let's check our answers:

__ 1. Score 1 point if you said "Mixter & Mondo." They're the only made-up PS2 duo on the page. And take away one point if you thought, *What's a PS2?*

__ 2. Score 1 point if you answered "Tartar sauce!" And if it's really 2050 and you're wondering, "Who is this SpongeBob you speak of?" he was a yellow sponge cartoon character … he talked, often saying things like "tartar sauce" … kids found him hilarious … so did many childish adults … like me. So there.

__ 3. Score 1 point if you chose *A Black Cat Named Bob*. All the others (plus loads more) are real TV shows about witches, vampires, and the occult. Spooky.

__ 4. Score 1 point if you circled "False." The scariest stat so far … according to recent research, one in 12 kids is no longer a virgin by his or her 13th birthday.

__ 5. On to lighter subjects … snack foods. Score 1 point if you checked "Fruit Gushers." I just made up the rest.

__ 6. Score 1 point if you answered "False." The real deal on Pokèmon is that it spiked in popularity among fourth- to sixth-grade boys in the late nineties, then waned. But it's recently made a comeback among younger first- to third-grade boys.

__ 7. Score 1 point if you chose "Cleanup." Cleanup is made up, but all the rest are real Pokèmon. Well … not "real." I mean, you're not going to see one walking down the street or anything. By "real" I mean … well … you know what I mean.

__ 8. Score 1 point if you picked "Pink hair." However, if you've jumped ahead and already read about *Lazytown* in chapter 10, then subtract 1 point for general sneakiness.

9. Score 1 point if you said "Dual Screen." Yes, this handheld game system has a screen for each eye. Pass the Ritalin.

10. Score 1 point if you said "Magnetic clothes." These pocket-sized fashionistas can now change clothes with a click. Like anyone really needs to change clothes that fast. I mean, where's the fire?

Total

Okay, time to separate the children from the adults. And by children, I mean really immature people.

If you scored 8 or higher: Congratulations! You are kid-savvy and culturally tapped in! (Or, if it's actually 2050, you may have a weird obsession with retro fads from the early part of the century.)

If you scored between 3 and 7: Not too shabby, but you're clearly not watching enough television. You may want to consider quitting your job to devote more hours to channel surfing PBS and the Disney Channel.

If you scored 2 or lower: Eek. You're hereby banished to hang out at Chuck E. Cheese's until further notice.

Okay, enough fun and games. Seriously ... what's with all the relevance? Yes, we all agree that it helps to be vaguely familiar with the world kids live in. Kids are our target audience, after all. But being relevant in children's ministry goes way beyond being able to use the words "tartar sauce" in a sentence.

Kids are an increasingly tough audience. While the kindergarteners and most of the first graders will still hang on every word you say, increasingly, you have to earn the right to be listened to by kids age eight and up. I'm not saying it's right; I'm just saying it's true.

These kids live in a tough world. More than half of them will spend this weekend at mom's place and next weekend at dad's. Theirs is a world in which having sex before 13 is far from unheard of; using the *F-word* with regularity is just part of being a normal fourth grader; and an endless onslaught of violence is just a game controller away.

Too often in children's ministry we paint an "everything is beautiful when you're a Christian" picture, and yet, like it or not, this is far from

pretend world

Sunday school Police
3.14159
2653589793

YOU SHOULD SEE THE OTHER GUY.

REAL WORLD WARNING — DO NOT IGNORE!!

the day-to-day reality for most kids. By tapping into kid culture, we let kids know that we're really tuned into the messy world they live in, and we earn the right to tell them all about the God who has answers in the midst of the mess.

Staying relevant also gives your teaching incredible power. It's one thing to say "video games ... bad ... stay away from video games." It's a whole new ball game when, in the midst of a lesson, you can refer in detail to the seventh level of *Twisted Metal 2.*

Suddenly . . . . BOOM!

Every kid just tuned in. You've got them all, especially the boys, right where you want them. By getting specific about real kid culture, you gain new respect and credibility in their eyes. You've set a powerful platform for when you pull out the Bible and start talking about what God has to say about living real life.

The bummer of bummers is that the culture is constantly changing. How can us big people keep up? No, you don't have to quit your job and go work at Chuck E. Cheese's.

Not unless you want to.

Here are five simple ways to soak up kid culture that will keep you plugged in and positioned for power.

TUNE IN

Tap into the heartbeat of the generation by tuning into kid-targeted TV. Watch kids' shows. Be the first one in line when the new Pixar movie comes out. TiVo *Lazytown* every day. Scope out *SpongeBob SquarePants.* Beneath his spongy square exterior, you'll find the stuff of genius. With Jedi-like ability, these shows ride into town each day like the ice-cream man on the hottest day of July, and the kids come a-running.

This ploy for more tube time goes way past just learning the who's who of popular television shows. So you know who SpongeBob SquarePants is. Big whoop. Take your TV-watching to the next step.

As you take in all these great kids' shows, move out of the spectator seat and watch from a practitioner's perspective. As a practitioner of reaching kids, scrutinize the show critically, looking for what works and what doesn't. Watch the show with kids and pay attention to how they react. Become a student, not just a viewer.

SpongeBob is funny. True, but any five-year-old could tell me that. Tell me *why*. If you can figure that out, you've discovered something useful that you can bring to your Bible lessons or incorporate into your teaching style. In the case of SpongeBob, you'll see that the show's silly, quirky style of humor is masterful. It's a barometer of what kids consider funny.

Scrutinize an episode of *Lazytown* and you'll be struck by how energetic the show is. But *why*? One reason: they use music and sound effects to energize the story. This is key learning in the quest to reach and teach kids.

The creators of kid-targeted television and movies are masters of their craft. They make it their business to know kids. And believe it or not, if we want to truly mesmerize kids with the power of the Bible, these masterminds have a few lessons to teach us.

So tune in. Yes, you'll be able to carry on intelligent conversations with your kids about the likes of Squidward and Plankton (okay, "intelligent" may be overstating it), but more importantly, you'll learn hard-won lessons from the kid-creativity gurus. Before long, you'll be soaking up creative, kid-friendly ideas like ... well ... like a sponge.

GET COMMERCIALLY CONNECTED

Short on time? Well, start your stopwatch. Here's the perfect time-saving technique for you. Click the remote to a kid channel (that would be PBS, Nickelodeon, The Disney Channel, or Noggin), and wait for the commercials.

Yep, you heard right. Commercials. In 60 seconds or less, you'll find out from the ad experts what cereals kids are eating, what snacks they love, and what toys they want.

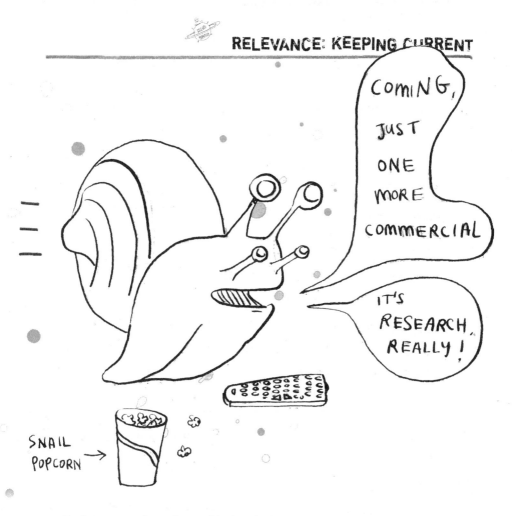

SNAIL POPCORN →

By knowing these bits of kid-trivia, you are positioned to send kids ongoing signals that you know their world. All this buy-in leads to power when it comes time to crack the Bible and talk heart-to-heart about God.

Remember the Fruit Gushers question? How did I know that secret source of info? From commercials. So when I have a game show about Jonah in next week's lesson, guess what I'll use for prizes? You guessed it. Fruit Gushers galore. That's an easy blip on the relevance meter. There's much more behind that prize than a slight sugar buzz ... they'll get a subtle signal that I know their world. And that translates into respect when, later in the lesson, I start talking about how Jonah disobeyed on the whole Nineveh deal and how they need to obey God even when it's hard. If they think I'm clueless about what their own personal Nineveh really looks like, then my teaching is sunk.

This type of 60-second research also sets you up to use specific examples in your teaching that bring a lesson to life. Compare these two different versions from a lesson on Abraham, targeted at a K–2 crowd.

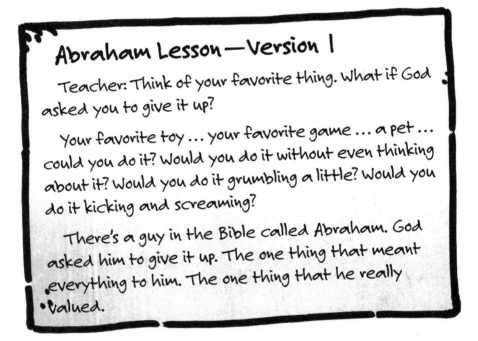

Abraham Lesson—Version 1

Teacher: Think of your favorite thing. What if God asked you to give it up?

Your favorite toy ... your favorite game ... a pet ... could you do it? Would you do it without even thinking about it? Would you do it grumbling a little? Would you do it kicking and screaming?

There's a guy in the Bible called Abraham. God asked him to give it up. The one thing that meant everything to him. The one thing that he really valued.

Analysis? Nice lead-in but very general. Nonspecific. Check out the same couple paragraphs with a little commercial-enhanced specificity.

GIVE UP A PET? WHO COULD EVER GIVE UP A FACE LIKE THIS?

Abraham Lesson — Version 2

Teacher: Think of your favorite thing. What if God asked you to give it up?

Your brand new "My Little Pony" Butterfly Island ... your Xbox 360 ... your dog ... could you do it? Would you do it without even thinking about it? Would you do it grumbling a little? Would you do it kicking and screaming?

There's a guy in the Bible called Abraham. God asked him to give it up. The one thing that meant everything to him. The one thing that he really valued.

Almost identical to the first version ... but as soon as you say "My Little Pony" Butterfly Island, every little girl in the room perked up and took notice, because they all either have this toy or want it. Every boy in the room took serious offense at the prospect of giving up the Xbox 360. And you want me to give up my dog? Forget about it.

The lesson is no longer theory. Suddenly you're hitting very close to home and now they're listening. Primed and ready for transformation. All that from a 60-second commercial.

SCORE BIG WITH VIDEO GAMES

Poor video games. So misunderstood. They get such a bad rap. Oh, don't get me wrong, there are some baddies out there. Full of excessive violence ... or worse. But those bad apples have spoiled the bunch in the eyes of so many of us.

As you know by now, I'm an avid video game player. But my video game obsession isn't driven by immaturity. Not totally, anyway. Part of my passion for this pixilated pastime is the power it gives me to draw boys into my Bible lessons and to speak directly to their hearts.

If a way to a man's heart is through his stomach, a way to a boy's heart is through his Wii. Mom, want to bond with your son? Show up after school with a Blockbuster rental in hand and play video games with him. I guarantee you'll be the most popular mother in the Northern Hemisphere. You'll speak his language, give value to something he finds important, and take your relationship to a whole new level.

Video games are a powerful inroad to life-changing Bible teaching with kids, especially with boys. It's easy for us to bad-mouth video games in general, especially when we've never played them. But we need to know what we're talking about if we want to equip kids. So play on. Then make your judgment call. When we rail about the evils of a particular video game and kids ask, "Have you ever played it?" and we say, "Well ... no." Ouch. We just lost all the credibility we had.

Versus saying, "God has got things to say about what we put into our minds.... He has specific things to say about what we fill up our hearts and minds with. How many of you guys have played *Megaroid: Dark Legacy?*"

The reference is specific ... every boy in the room just leaned in.

"You know when you get to the ending boss battle of level two, and you defeat him, your guy chops his head off, right? Oh, it's disgusting."

I've got the ear of every boy in the room. They're all thinking "This guy knows what he's talking about. He knows my world. He's really played this game." Every one of them is listening. I now have credibility when I go on to say ...

"God has got something to say to you about that game. It's not good to put those images in your mind. Check out Philippians 4:8 ... it says 'Whatever is true, whatever is noble, whatever is right, whatever is pure, whatever is lovely, whatever is admirable ... if anything is excellent or praiseworthy—think about such things.' God has stuff to say about this scene in *Megaroid: Dark Legacy*, and if we want to truly call ourselves followers of God, then we need to challenge ourselves about what we regularly choose to fill up our heads with."

And when they ask if I've played it, I can stand before them and say, "Yeah, I played it. I got all the way up to level two. Then I had a choice to make. And I decided it was time to shut the system down, because I knew that God's got stuff to say about this."

Wow. Nothing speaks loud and clear like the voice of experience.

Nice score.

FLIP PAGES

Magazines are a gold mine of cultural relevance. Because they come out monthly, they are a constant update to what's hot and what's not. Two of my favorites are *Disney Adventures* and *Nickelodeon Magazine*.

Pressed for time to stay connected? Just subscribing to one (or both) of these will take all the work out of keeping current in kid biz. It'll show up in your mailbox each month, all ready to be read on the morning train commute or scanned over your lunch break. You'd be amazed how much of an update you'll get in just a quick flip-through.

In a ten-minute page flipping session (literally ... ten minutes) of this month's issue of *Disney Adventures Magazine*, here's all the kid-friendly tidbits that I unearthed:

- *Kingdom Hearts II* (hot new PS2 game) hits shelves this month. I should rent it and give it a test-drive with my son this weekend.
- The star of the new mermaid movie *Aquamarine* is a cool new face to the big screen named Jojo. Good to know. Girls will have their eye on her as a potential role model.
- The fantasy book series *The Edge Chronicles* is hotter than ever with boys and girls alike. Add to my "books to read" list.
- *The Chronicles of Narnia* comes out on DVD this month. The mag devoted three separate articles and a quiz to the movie, indicating that it's still *hot, hot, hot.*
- A full-color spread on the *Judy Moody* books by Megan McDonald tells me that these books are still big hits with kids.
- *Ice Age 2* hit theaters a couple weeks ago. Most kids will have seen it before the month is out.
- There's a visual brainteaser puzzle in the "Befuddles" section, and it is hard to figure out! This tells me that kids love complicated puzzles like this, and I should make my game shows challenging.

Not a bad take-home from a ten-minute skim over lunch.

A steady bite-sized diet of magazines like this will keep you on the inside track of popular kid culture, and equip you with easy movie references, video game knowledge, and creative ideas for new game shows and lesson ideas. But remember ... it's not just about the pop culture. All of this relevant data provides you with kid buy-in, giving you awesome inroads for potent Bible teaching. That's a lunchtime regimen that's worth sticking to.

RAAAWK! POLLY WANTS A STEADY BITE-SIZED DIET OF MAGAZINES! RAAAAAWK!

BE A FRY ON THE WALL

There's no better way to hear real-life kid conversation in action than hanging out around kids and listening in. A playground is a good choice, but let's face it, a 30-something-year-old guy hanging out alone by the swings in the park is just creepy.

So I hang out at McDonalds. It so happens that I spend a good bit of my writing time hunkered down in a booth at Mickey D's. What can I say? A place where I can plug in my laptop and get an all-day IV of Diet Coke? I'm there. But there's more appeal to this fast food hangout for me than the free flow of caffeine. The joint is a kid magnet. When it comes to hearing kids speak when they think nobody's listening, this is a great place.

FLY SPIES

DID YOU CATCH THAT?

RECORDED

Zoom

CLICK

CLICK

SUPER FRIES

How do I know that the *F-word* features prominently in a typical fourth-grader's vocabulary, especially when they think no adults are listening? McDonald's. After school, freed from the watchful eyes of parents and teachers, mounted on bikes of every stripe, fourth and fifth graders gather in droves at my local golden arches. And the *F-word* flies freely. Understand something … this isn't the McDonald's just off the Sodom and Gomorrah interchange (though, if these towns were still open for business, I'm sure they'd have one). Nope, this is a typical suburb in Midwest America.

As much as I may not like these facts about this potty-mouth epidemic, I'm glad I know. It puts me closely in touch with the kids I regularly teach. This is the real world kids live in ... including Christian kids. These are the cold, brutal facts. And if I want to speak into kid reality and teach for true transformation, I need to know them.

But hanging out at this cheeseburger paradise does more than give me a front row seat to the corruption of our youth. It's also a great place to hear more uplifting conversation in action, being bantered around by kids of every age. By planting myself squarely in the sidelines of the McDonald PlayPlace, I'm an ear-witness to the lingo and language of the day.

If you write your own lessons or drama scripts, the PlayPlace is the happenin' hot-spot for picking up the real words and phrases that come out of kids' mouths. This type of authenticity helps your scripts ring true. It also keeps you current on language you may want to weave into your teaching. Let's face it, kids can smell a fake a mile away. Throwing the phrase "the bomb" into your lesson, when no kid has said that in six months, well ... the only thing more fake than that is the shark from *Jaws*.

JORDAN'S FACE HAS BEEN MASKED TO PROTECT HIS IDENTITY

Stylish sayings come and go very quickly. Regularly surrounding yourself with real-kid banter at places like McDonald's helps you relate naturally and authentically to the kids you teach. You'll hear them talking about things that matter to them, in words that they really use.

All that, and an occasional hot apple pie. I'm lovin' it.

159 MILLION BILLION ZILLION SERVED

How'd you do?

How well did you understand this chapter?
Take our quiz and find out!

1.  is to ... as ... is to ...

a. ... b. ... c. ... d. ...

2. What is the capital of Uzbekistan?

CHANGING DIAPERS? CHANGING LIVES!

PRESCHOOL PRINCIPLES

Sunday morning.

Miss Katie is trying desperately to enrapture her pre-K class with the story of Jonah and the Whale. But four-year-old James just got a new kitty and insists on announcing it over and over at the top of his lungs. Little Trevor just learned how to blow his own nose and is demonstrating for his neighbors. And three-and-a-half-year-old Samantha needs to go potty.

No doubt ... when it comes to teaching the Bible, the pre-K crowd is fraught with its own unique challenges and struggles.

While I've spent much of my teaching tenure in the land of K through five, I've logged enough time in front of the pre-K crowd to know one thing for sure ... the preschool ministry's rep for being "the easy side of Sunday school" is a bad rap. These peanuts are one tough crowd. In fact, effectively reaching kids between two and five may be the toughest of all tasks when it comes to teaching the Bible creatively.

If we could rub the diaper genie and make a wish, it would probably be for some solid and successful techniques for transforming our pre-K teaching time from exhausting to exhilarating. That, and an endless supply of fish crackers.

Well, there's not much I can do about your snack-time dilemma, but when it comes to tangible teaching techniques, your wish is granted. I've had the pleasure of working closely with volunteers who were masters at making an impact on Sunday school's shortest customers. Rubbing shoulders with these early-childhood champions has taught me tons.

Additionally, I've become a sponge when it comes to soaking up skills from the experts in preschool-targeted television. My learnings? Several A-B-C's for teaching the Bible to the under-six set that truly have the power to turn preschool anarchy into pint-sized awe.

weee!

SESAME STREET SECRETS
(BROUGHT TO YOU BY THE LETTER S)

In November of 1969, a new kind of show aired on television.

Its purpose? To "make a difference in the lives of (young) children, in particular, poor inner-city children, and help prepare them for school."[1] In short, to teach basic educational concepts to preschoolers.

Its format? An hour-long daily program that would capitalize on "rapid-fire pace, slick production, and catchy music."[2]

It's name? *Sesame Street.*

It was an instant hit. In fact, in one season *Sesame Street* became synonymous with outstanding children's television. And 37 years later, it's still zipping along strong. In the face of such unparalleled success, such uncanny ability to enrapture children, such untethered imagination, I am left wondering one thing about the creators of this American icon.

Were those psychos totally out of their gourds?

Think about it. What they were taking on had never been attempted. Not just an *educational television show* for kids. That was gutsy enough. But these crazies created an *hour-long* educational television show *targeted at preschoolers*!

Impossible.

Unthinkable.

It should never have worked.

But, armed with irrefutable research, incredible talent, and an unshakable plan to test out their materials on real kids before it ever hit the screen, they did it. And dominated.

So, since we in children's ministry find ourselves inconveniently without the magic of Jim Henson, Joe Raposo, and the rest of the *Sesame Street* masterminds to aid our efforts, is there a juicy tidbit or two we can extract from *Sesame Street* that will help us reach preschoolers with the Bible?

You bet your sweet Snuffleupagus there is. No magic required.

Though "A-la-peanut-butter-sandwiches" is still pretty fun to say.

Magazine-Style Format

One thing the *Sesame Street* gurus knew—small, short snippets were essential ingredients to make the content appetizing to preschoolers. Shortly before the first show aired, Joan Ganz Cooney, the smarts behind the whole *Sesame Street* idea, put it this way in an interview with the *New York Times*: "Traditional educators may not be nuts about this, but we're going to clip along at a much faster pace than anyone's used to in children's programs. [Kids] like commercials and banana-peel humor.... We have to infuse our content into forms children find accessible."

ADULT ATTENTION SPAN →

And so, a typical show opens with a four-minute segment between Maria and Big Bird on Sesame Street,

then switches to a 1-minute animation about the number 12,

then moves to a live-action sequence between Grover and a small child talking about cooperation,

and so on ...

This is the magazine-style format at its finest. These short, self-contained bites acknowledge, without apology, that little kids have little attention spans.

Start by keeping your total teaching time to a minimum, 15 to 20 minutes max. Then break that time into short little snippets ...

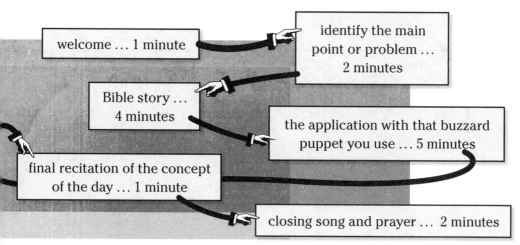

welcome ... 1 minute

identify the main point or problem ... 2 minutes

Bible story ... 4 minutes

the application with that buzzard puppet you use ... 5 minutes

final recitation of the concept of the day ... 1 minute

closing song and prayer ... 2 minutes

... for example.

Grand total ... 15 minutes. Just long enough. Little Zachary hasn't quite had enough time to get bored and start eating the wallpaper. Help that teaching time zip along by building it from small little segments and teeny bites that three-year-olds can sink their baby teeth into.

LITTLE KID ATTENTION SPAN:

Characters with Character

Sesame Street has long been the place where an odd but approachable assortment of characters live. From monsters, to frogs, to grouches, to ... whatever Bert and Ernie are ... they're the people that you meet when you're walking down the street.

Originally, the many characters of *Sesame Street* were not going to actually live on the Street but only appear in taped segments between the street stuff. But thanks to the *Sesame* research team, they discovered that the kids lost interest when the Muppets weren't there. Good thing too. Can you imagine *Sesame Street* without Oscar in the can? Big Bird on his nest? The Twiddlebugs in the window box?

Sesame Street showed the world that "real" people and quirky characters can, maybe even should, coexist. But there are a few rules to the craft of using characters that can bring great power to your own ministry neighborhood.

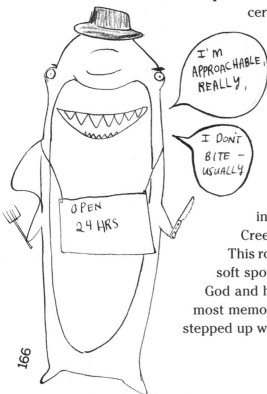

Keep characters approachable. While they're certainly unusual, every character on the Street is *approachable*. Even the Grouch. Even the monsters. I mean, come on, they've even got a vampire, for counting out loud. But they're all approachable ... loveable even. That's an important part of character success with the preschool gang.

Tom Nagy is a burly brawny carpenter who has been serving in the preschool ministry at Willow Creek Community Church for 17 years. This rough-and-tumble guy has a serious soft spot for teaching preschoolers about God and has played some of the ministry's most memorable characters. It was Tom who stepped up when the ministry writers invented a new character, a pumped-up strong man named Melvin the Muscleman. Decked out in a sweatshirt stuffed to the seams with foam balls, Tom, as Melvin, entered the scene to pump up the kids' faith.

> "It was a disaster," Tom says. "I was just too intimidating for them. A couple weeks later we tried having me put my muscles into the sweatshirt in front of the kids, so they'd see that it was just me ... but that just got goofy."

So Melvin the Muscleman bit the dust. And with good reason. Melvin wasn't approachable enough. Maybe it would have worked if Melvin had been cast as a pumped-up puppet instead of a fully grown man. Any parent who's ever gone to Disney World and watched their kids freak out at the size of Goofy knows that full-grown characters can sometimes be awfully intimidating to a preschooler. Imagine Oscar as a six-foot-four Grouch. Stuff of nightmares.

Tom has a great take on the experience:

> "At the end of the lesson, kids almost always want to come up and hug the characters ... for a two-year-old who can't put a sentence together yet, a hug may be the only way to relate to this character ... to connect ... characters absolutely need to be approachable."

Childlike characters work. Many of the creatures that inhabit *Sesame Street* were conceived with this in mind. According to David Borgennicht in the great book *Sesame Street Unpaved*, Elmo is written as a three-year-old, Prairie Dawn is seven, and Grover psychologically represents a four-year-old. No wonder Super-Grover can't seem to manage a smooth landing.

What's with all the child's play? Preschool power-player Tom Nagy says: "The character is the voice of the kids." Well, Melvin the Muscleman may have missed the mark, but Tom's hitting the bulls-eye.

Childlike characters help kids work through the topic, often asking the same questions kids are thinking about. Whether a live character or a fuzzy-headed puppet, these characters give a teacher a great foil, a way to teach kids indirectly (by teaching the character) without just talking at them.

One of Tom's newest characters, Cowboy Cole, takes this concept a step further. Not stupid by any stretch, this slow-on-the-draw dude just takes his time working things out. Most times, the kids have lassoed the answer and are already shouting it out while poor ol' Cole is still thinking it through. But that's okay. By knowing a little more than Cole, the kids feel empowered. Helping Cole wrangle the right conclusion gives the kids more ownership of the content themselves.

Characters need a "real" person to help them work things out. *Sesame Street* does this all the time, but never better than the day that Mr. Hooper died. When actor Will Lee died of cancer in 1982, rather than recasting the role, the brave *Sesame Street* gang chose to deal with his death head on. And as Big Bird, the eternal four-year-old, grappled with understanding this painful concept and the loss of his friend, it was Maria, Susan, and Bob, the humans on the *Street* who stood by him and tried to help him make sense of it all.

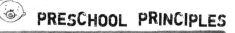

Characters work best when there's a real person there to help work things out. This doesn't imply that characters should always be bumbling and dopey, in need of being set straight by the all-knowing all-wise teacher. It just means that, when it comes to driving the main concept home, when making sense of the Bible and life, a "real" person gives the content credibility.

I'm all for a puppet buzzard or a talking dresser raising questions or working problems out. I just wouldn't advocate for a talking piece of furniture leading kids across the line of faith. That crosses some odd fantasy/reality lines that are hard to put my finger on, but that I know are there nonetheless. Even flesh-and-blood human characters, like Cowboy Cole, need to be balanced by a "real" person, a teacher who isn't up there being anybody but herself.

LESSONS FROM *LAZYTOWN*

In 2004, Nick Jr. launched a brand-new powerhouse in its lineup, jam-packed with cool characters and plenty of va-va-voom.

Imported from Iceland, *Lazytown* instantaneously raised the bar on making "healthy living" exciting to kids. Taking on topics like "playing outside versus video games," "getting enough sleep," "not eating junk food," and geared toward the late preschool crowd, this Scandinavian success immediately had kids of all ages eating carrot sticks right out of their hands.

What can a show about health teach us in children's ministry? Sit up and take notice.

LAZYTOWN, EH? SOUNDS LIKE MY KIND OF PLACE.

169

Say It, Don't Spray It

Often in children's ministry we live by the "more is more" principle. We want kids to know so much about God we spray them with information—like a sprinkler gone haywire. We think if we just say it all then they'll get it. But the truth is, the more we pack into a single lesson, the less kids walk out with.

Lazytown is masterful at "less for more" thinking. Over the course of the season, *Lazytown* covers a wide scope of topics, but each story-driven episode focuses on a single clear learning objective. In one show, the whole point is that Sportacus, the spandex-shrouded hero, goes to sleep at exactly 8:08 every night. In another, Stephanie, Sportacus' pink-haired compatriot, discovers a memorable formula for brushing her teeth: 20 times up, 20 times down, 20 times left, 20 times right. And while I saw these episodes months ago, I remember them like they were yesterday. And so do my kids. That's the power of "less for more" teaching.

Let every part of Sunday's lesson—the Bible story, the application, the verse, the small group or circle-time, even the craft and snack (if possible)—all orbit around *one concept*. This is "less for more" teaching.

If you're going to teach "don't lie," then just teach "don't lie." You don't have to get into the fact that

> oh, by the way, this is only one of ten other commandments,
>
> and while I'm at it let me briefly mention the other nine,
>
> and now that you mention it, you're probably all wondering how Moses got up that hill in the first place,
>
> and "what's adultery?" you ask? Ummmm ...

One clear concept. If you're three years old, it's enough for you to know that God doesn't want you to lie because lying hurts people. So don't lie. I'm not much for fortune cookie wisdom, especially when it comes to the Bible, but if you can't fit your Bible truth onto a fortune cookie paper, then you may be trying to teach too much. And writing really small doesn't count. And using a fortune cookie the size of a Volkswagen doesn't count either. Normal-sized fortune cookie.

So resist the urge to spray kids down with a shower of truth. You'll find that a clear, simple concept, taught in a memorable way, will hit home with the impact of a fire hose.

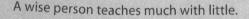

> A wise person teaches much with little.

> Fewer concepts bring many joys.

> Eat at Joe's Wok!

Get a Handle on Things

Not only is *Lazytown* teaching fewer concepts for more retention, but they use memorable handles that help kids hold on to the concepts. Handles are visual or memorable ways to help kids grip the concept or go where we want to take them.

"Get plenty of rest" is such a forgettable phrase. But the idea of going to bed at 8:08 is clear, specific, and incredibly memorable ... a great handle. The "20 times" rule of teeth-brushing is not only fun but unforgettable. Just last night, a *year and a half* after my daughter and I first saw the teeth-brushing episode of *Lazytown*, I heard her in front of the mirror, counting to 20 as she brushed. She's done it every night since she saw Sportacus do it. *Lazytown* gave my daughter a handle on how to brush her teeth.

Make that one clear concept—that little juicy nugget that you want kids to chant repeatedly in the car the whole way home, driving their parents slowly but surely into a state of total psychosis—make it a phrase that's easily repeatable. In fact, say it several times throughout the lesson, and have the kids say it with you. Tell the story of Peter lying about being Jesus' friend with the recurring phrase ...

"Lying hurts ... *OW!* ... so do not lie!"

Great little handle. Saying the "OW!" part is fun, and it gives kids a memorable way to hold on to this truth.

Handles can also help gain attention and guide kids through the teaching experience. Kerri Mahla, a friend and preschool sensei extraordinaire, goes through a weekly ritual with the kids called "putting on their listening ears." At the top of every teaching time, Kerri leads her vertically challenged charges in an elaborate ceremony that involves attaching imaginary ears onto their heads, yanking on each earlobe repeatedly, while "click-clock-click-clocking" with her tongue, thus ratcheting their listening ears up from "casually interested" mode into the "I love listening to Miss Kerri more than all the ice cream in the world" setting.

Not only do the kids adore this weekly rite, but should Kerri forget to have them put on their listening ears, she's in for the scolding of the century. And if you've ever been scolded by a three-year-old, then you know what a vexing encounter that can be.

This ear-tugging routine is a simple handle ... a way of helping these kids grab on and get ready for listening, without having to say, "No one talks when Miss Kerri is talking." Such rules and lectures are so easy to ignore, but no one checks out when Miss Kerri is putting on the listening ears.

The habit of putting easy-grab handles on concepts doesn't apply only during teaching time. What about when you gather kids into small groups or circle-time? The other day I saw some sassy little mouse pads at IKEA. For 50 cents apiece! They had funky little turquoise and lime green circles on them ... very fun. I've seen similar ones at Target for under a buck. Rather than using them for computer-related pursuits as they were intended, what if you buy enough of those mouse pads for every kid in the ministry, and when it's time to move into circle-time or small groups, every kid grabs one and uses it as a little seat? You could rename your small-group time "The Mouse Pad." Then, rather than saying, "Trevor, sit still," or "Judy, stay seated," you could remind those little tykes that the only ones who get to share at "The Mouse Pad" are the ones who have their bottoms on their mouse pads and their lips as quiet as mice. It gives them a visual handle to hold on to, one that helps them do exactly what you want them to do. There's something special about each kid having his or her own mouse pad that makes it a joyful privilege to keep their butt cheeks attached to it.

DORA AND BLUE'S FORMULA FOR SUCCESS

Dora the Explorer. It's not a very good rhyme. Dora … explorer. But ask any preschooler and they'll say it again,

    and again,

    and again,   *and again, and again, and again, and again, and again, and again*

    and again …

    It's a great show.

    Blue's Clues. Same deal, but with this one, the rhyme's a little better. The fan base remains firm: *Top notch programming. Can't get enough. Four ✕★✕★ stars.*

Dora and Blue have discovered an amazing recipe for success. But it's not due to unbelievable special effects, groundbreaking animation, or unheard-of educational principles. So what makes these two shows blockbuster hits with the under-K club?

    It's all in the formula.

The Facts about Formula

I don't know if you've noticed, but every episode of *Blue's Clues* and *Dora the Explorer* is exactly the same. Maddeningly so.

Episode after episode, Dora and her monkey-buddy Boots need to get somewhere. They look at the map and the talking parchment tells them where to go …

UND HERE VEE HAVE EIN FORMULA FÜR SUCCESS!

☐ INTRO

← POUCH (ALWAYS HANDY)

Bubble Bridge!
Muddy Mountain!
Gooey Geyser!
Bubble Bridge!
Muddy Mountain!
Gooey Geyser!
Bubble Bridge!

Show after show, Blue the dog sends her buddy Joe hot on the trail to discover three clues.

Oh, sure, the content changes from show to show. This time Dora is headed for the Gooey Geyser, next time it's Crocodile Lake. This time Blue's clues lead to making lemonade, next time they indicate that Joe's little indigo pup wants to go to the library. But beyond minor content changes, every single episode follows the exact same formula.

Brilliance. Pure brilliance.

What's so smart about formula? It plays right into the hands of an important fact ... young kids love to be *in the know* but rarely are. Three- and-four-year-olds love it that, time after time, Joe goes in red-hot pursuit of those paw-print-covered clues, only to walk right past them. You'd think poor Joe would catch on by now, but nope. He always misses them, and the kids watching at home have to point them out. Kids love knowing that, after Joe draws that third and final clue in his handy-dandy notebook, he's heading for the Thinking Chair. This kind of unwavering repetitious formula creates a predictable and wonderful world that kids can see coming.

We often think we have to keep things changing, to keep the kids guessing. And at the elementary-age levels, we're right on the money ... variety is the name of the game. But when teaching a roomful of two-and-up tots, formula creates uncanny interest and attention. They know what's coming next, and they're *waiting* for it to happen.

I know. You're thinking, *"Formula? You want me to do the same thing every week?"*

Yep. Same set, same order of elements, same characters, same, same, same.

"Won't the kids get tired of that?"

Does your preschool son ever get tired of watching *Dora*? Ask him. The answer is "Quiet, Mom, I'm watching *Dora*."

"But how long can a single formula sustain itself?"

I've seen ministries run the exact same formula for a year straight with great success.

"A year?"

Yep.

"A whole year?"

Is there an echo in here? Yeah, a year. Easily.

"So what does a formula like this look like?"

That's the question I've been waiting for! It could look like this:

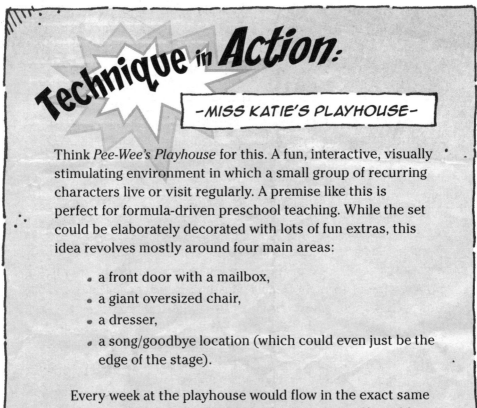

Technique in *Action:*

—MISS KATIE'S PLAYHOUSE—

Think *Pee-Wee's Playhouse* for this. A fun, interactive, visually stimulating environment in which a small group of recurring characters live or visit regularly. A premise like this is perfect for formula-driven preschool teaching. While the set could be elaborately decorated with lots of fun extras, this idea revolves mostly around four main areas:

- a front door with a mailbox,
- a giant oversized chair,
- a dresser,
- a song/goodbye location (which could even just be the edge of the stage).

Every week at the playhouse would flow in the exact same order. For up to a year solid. Only the content itself would change. Here's a rundown of the formula for Miss Katie's Playhouse ...

CONTINUED!

1. Welcome and Set Up the Problem

Miss Katie comes in through the front door. She's not a character, she's herself … the teacher. She welcomes the kids to the playhouse, maybe performing some type of "get ready for the fun" ritual each week like putting on listening ears. She takes a letter out of the mailbox. Every week there's a letter from a different friend. The letter describes a problem and wonders if God or the Bible has an answer for it.

So maybe this week, the letter reads:

> Dear Miss Katie,
> My dumb old brother wouldn't share his beanbag chair with me today. I was so mad that I didn't give him any of my leftover Easter bunny when he asked me. I just stuffed it all in my mouth … no sharing! Now it's like were not even friends. Does your favorite book, the Bible, have anything in there to help us?
> Your friend, Becky

You betcha, Becky! As a matter of fact, it does.

Bam!… The kids have been welcomed, and the problem has been identified. The stage is set for some great teaching in a creative, yet predictable way that the kids expect each week.

CONTINUED!

2. StoryChair

Remember that big oversized chair I mentioned? Here's where it makes its debut. After the mailbox routine, Miss Katie goes to the StoryChair, pulls out her big oversized Bible, and tells the story. Just like Joe and his Thinking Chair on *Blue's Clues*, the kids always know that Miss Katie goes to the StoryChair to tell the story. They're waiting for it.

But just because she's sitting in the StoryChair doesn't mean she has to just *read* the story. Remember, think visually. Think kinesthetically. This is one of those places that you can bring in some simple variation. While she *always* goes to the StoryChair to tell the story, maybe some weeks a familiar character comes by for a visit (like Cowboy Cole or Zuzzy the buzzard puppet), and they help her tell or reenact the story. The big oversized chair is a perfect place for a puppeteer to hide behind. It's also a great place for Miss Katie to stash some cool props, and maybe she uses those to help visually tell the story. Or maybe Miss Katie invites some kids up into the Playhouse from the audience, and they help tell the story.

A little variety in the storytelling from week to week is great here, because it's imbedded within the formula ... the StoryChair. As long as Miss Katie always goes to the chair to tell the story, and as long as you limit the cast of characters

CONTINUED!

NORMAL SIZE BIBLE

HOLY BIBLE

MISS KATIE'S ← GIANT BIBLE

OOF!

178

that occasionally visit the Playhouse to a few familiar ones (or even just one!), the power of the formula stays on track.

So maybe this week ...

Miss Katie tells the story of the Rich Young Ruler. Jesus wanted the man to share what he had because that would show how much he loved Jesus. But the man loved his stuff more than he loved Jesus, so he couldn't share. Cowboy Cole stops by just as Miss Katie's sitting in the StoryChair, and he helps her by playing out the Rich Young Ruler, not wanting to share his ten-gallon cowboy hat, his super-squirt water pistol, and his stick horse, Matilda.

Again, simple stuff. But it plays up the power of a great character. It makes the story visual. We're following a magazine-style format, moving from element (mailbox) to element (StoryChair). In short, we're creating a lesson that is simple and do-able but teaches in a way preschoolers really respond to.

3. Dresser Time

Miss Katie's Playhouse is kind of a zany place to be. In addition to a cool mailbox that gets letters from friends and a really big StoryChair, there's also a talking dresser. And every week, after the story is told from the StoryChair, the kids are just waiting for the moment when Dresser opens his eyes and starts talking.

Again, this is very reminiscent of *Pee-Wee's Playhouse*, which had a talking chair and map and who knows what all else. Let's face it, talking furniture is just fun stuff. Here's the anatomy of this dresser puppet ... you get an old dresser from a thrift store and paint it out in fun colors. Put eyes on it, either standard puppet eyes, or splurge (since you only have to do one cool set a year!) and get some eyes with a

CONTINUED!

mechanism that lets them blink. The third drawer is the mouth. Rip the back panel off the dresser, exposing the inside from the back. The puppeteer crouches behind the dresser, opening and closing the third drawer from the back. Instant (and cheap!) talking dresser.

Dresser is the childlike character that helps kids get to the application of the story. Miss Katie uses Dresser to bubble up specific ways kids can live out the one clear concept the Bible teaches each week.

So maybe this week ...

Dresser: *Great story, Miss Katie!*

Miss Katie: *Oh, hi, Dresser! Hey, everybody, it's Dresser. On the count of three, let's all say hi to Dresser in our special Playhouse way! Ready? One ... two ... three ... "Hi, Dresser! It's knobs to see you!"*

Dresser: *Knobs to see you guys too!*

Miss Katie: *So you were listening to the story of the Rich Man, huh?*

Dresser: *Well, trying to!*

Miss Katie: *Trying to?*

Dresser: *It was kind of hard to hear because ... the socks are fighting again.*

180

CONTINUED!

Miss Katie: *The socks?*

Dresser: *Yeah, the socks that live in my second drawer down.*

Miss Katie: *Fighting again, huh?*

Dresser: *Yep.*

Miss Katie: *About what?*

Dresser: *They both like to be on your right foot when you wear them.*

Miss Katie: *My right foot?*

Dresser: *Yep. They don't want to share that foot. The red sock says that she always should be on the right foot, and the yellow sock says that she gets the right foot. [Maybe Miss Katie always wears one red sock and one yellow sock.]*

Miss Katie: *All that over my right foot?*

Dresser: *Yep. They sure do love that foot.*

Miss Katie: *It sounds like it. It sounds like they love that foot more than they love each other.*

Dresser: *Wow … I never thought of it like that.*

Miss Katie: *Maybe I'd better take a break from wearing both of them for a little while.*

Dresser: *But Miss Katie! Then neither of them would get the right foot.*

Miss Katie: *Well, you heard the story, right … ?*

Dresser: *Mostly.*

Miss Katie: *Jesus showed us that sometimes we need to give up what we want, so that we can remind ourselves how much we love him … or each other.*

Dresser: *Give it up?*

Miss Katie: *Yep. Maybe if they both give up the right foot for a while, they'll remember that they love each other more than my smelly old foot.*

NG

CONTINUED!

Dresser: *Hey, yeah! But then what?*

Miss Katie: *Well, once they remember that they love each other and Jesus more than my foot, then they'll be ready to share!*

Dresser: *Yeah … like maybe they take turns on the right foot.*

Miss Katie: *That's a perfect way to share!*

Dresser: *Or maybe … you could wear them both on the right foot at the same time, and no sock on your left foot.*

Miss Katie: *I guess once in a while that would be okay!*

Dresser: *Or maybe they could switch off weeks. This week red gets the right, next week yellow gets it.*

Miss Katie: *Now you've got it! There's lots of ways to share. But first you have to be willing to let the stuff you love go. Remember, God wants us to love him first, people second …*

Dresser: *And stuff last!*

Miss Katie: *I like that! Let's say that together with our friends! Love God first! People second! Stuff last!*

You see where this is going. Dresser is a way to nail that application, giving specific ways the kids can live out the Bible story this week. Because Dresser Time is part of the formula (it always follows the StoryChair), the kids are glued in, waiting for him to talk. That's the power of formula! It pulls them in as they watch and wait for what they already know is coming.

And that little phrase—"Love God first! People second! Stuff last!"—is a great handle. Highly repeatable.

Love God first! People second! Stuff last!

4. Wrap Up and "So Long" Song

Our last stop in the Playhouse formula is an intimate final moment with the kids. It's a chance to remind them that we answered the letter we got from Becky. A chance to tell them one last time what it means for them to share this week. A chance to sing a goodbye song. And a chance to pray. You could have this in a special spot in Miss Katie's Playhouse, but I think just sitting on the edge of the stage makes it simpler and more intimate.

Now, if it's important to you to sing several songs each week, this could be the place to do it. But keep a short playlist, so that the kids always know the songs. As soon as you switch to a bunch of songs that they don't know, you'll lose them. And it's incredibly strong to pick one final song as your "so long song" and sing that one every week. You may think they'll get sick of it, but trust me, you'll have them eating right out of your hands.

In this Playhouse premise, Miss Katie can end by praying, and dismiss the kids to the next activity in the lineup.

Formulaic?

Totally. Completely. Unapologetically. And completely compelling to a pre-K kid.

Sesame Street. Lazytown. Dora the Explorer. Blue's Clues. These folks are experts at reaching preschool kids. What others call "kiddie programming," I call an early morning master class at reaching pre-K kids with the power of the Bible. Let's tune in to these compelling lessons with listening ears on.

HAPPINESS IS **183** SOCKS THAT ALL MATCH

Your preschool ministry may dwell in the back corner of the basement. But you are not a babysitter or a nanny. You are not a changer of diapers ... *you* are a changer of *lives*. You know that. I know that. God knows that. Even the three-year-olds know that.

Everyone else? Well ... they'll catch on eventually.

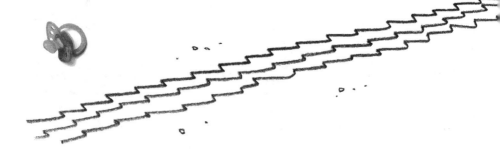

Chapter 10 Notes

1. Joan Ganz Cooney, quoted in David Borgenicht's *Sesame Street Unpaved* (New York: Hyperion Books, 1998), 9.

2. Borgenicht, *Sesame Street Unpaved*, 14.

5 ets and decor.
  Lights, video, and sound.

We all recognize these tools communicate tons to a generation of tech-savvy kids. But let's face it, many of us feel out of our league when it comes to decor dilemmas. Most of us feel woefully under-geeky when it comes to tech know-how.

No worries. The following pages are full-up with decor design principles for the uninspired and tech techniques to guide the most un-eggheaded.

DESIGNING DYNAMIC DIGS

Here's the truth of the matter: we often have to teach a wide age range all together. Whether or not it's our first choice, teaching combined K–5 lessons is common. So when it comes to creating decor or lesson themes that work, I live by a little rule:

COOL flows DOWNHILL.

Simply put, target the oldest boy in the room. If it's cool enough for him, it's cool enough for everyone else. It's a mistake to target the younger kids with decor or creative approaches because you'll strike out with everybody else. Even shooting for the middle kids leaves you missing the mark. The fifth-grade boy (or sixth-grade boy, if your children's ministry goes up that high) is your toughest customer.

Now, let's clarify … this rule doesn't dictate your *content* choices necessarily. In other words, you're not going to teach on the topic of evolution or purity to the wee-est ones just because you're targeting the oldest kid. Caution and prudence need to be applied when figuring out the content side of the equation. But when it comes to creating spaces that work, deciding creative approaches, or picking music, if you're combining grade levels … the "cool flows downhill" rule applies.

Girls are simply much more accommodating (sorry guys) and will respond well to a wide variety of choices. And younger kids want to be just like their older counterparts. It's the older boys who think they're too cool for school. They're assessing the space from the moment they walk in the door. Hook them, and you've hooked the room.

So let's cast off. Here are some decor techniques for designing a teaching space dynamic enough to hook the big ones.

To Theme or Not to Theme

Hey, I love an African Safari VBS as much as the next guy. Or a bug-themed summer unit. For special events like these, I say theme yourself silly. Go nuts.

But for the week-to-week teaching routine, you can make a powerful punch and save big bucks by creating generic looks rather than themed ones. When I use the word generic, don't start picturing a can with a black-and-white label with only the word "Corn" printed on the front. By *generic*, I don't mean "sterile," "boring," or "icky." I'm talking "all-purpose" set designs.

After all, that barnyard set is only going to have life for so long before you need to change it, right? And changing the set and decor for every teaching unit is time-consuming and costly. Not to mention that, when it comes to being on Old MacDonald's Farm, all you're gonna get from the older crowd is an "eye-roll" here and an "eye-roll" there.

Constantly changing themes drains tons of time and energy that could be better spent memorizing your lesson or working on your peaks and valleys.

But what about shelling out the bucks and energy one time for a stylin' *all-purpose* set? Now you've invested time and money wisely into a set that has a longer life and doesn't need to be changed every month.

My team and I once created a set for the fourth- and fifth-grade teaching room that had loads of all-purpose appeal. It had kind of a junkyard/back alley look ... a three-level painter's scaffold, garbage cans, piles of odds and ends, chain-link hanging in the background. We weren't trying to create a junkyard "theme," just a cool hip space in which we could do a variety of teaching. It was a perfect generic set; we could teach any story from this setting. When we told the story of Paul and Silas, the chain-link became the prison. When we did Jesus being tempted by Satan from the top of the temple, we climbed up the scaffold. When we wanted to teach David and Goliath using audience participation, the garbage cans were pre-stashed with swords and costume pieces, and Goliath stood on a stack of old tires from the garbage heap. As a bonus, the set was cut-rate to create because we made it mostly from junk we found around the church and in people's garages. It was the perfect permanent look for the teaching room. Any story could be taught in this space.

If you have all the people-power and money you need to change your teaching set into themed units each month, by all means, party on. But many of us continue the crazy-making themed-set-cycle because we think that's what kids crave. Not necessarily. By teaching from a cool all-purpose set each week, and suggesting the story with props or single costume pieces, we give the kids a chance to engage their imaginations. What could be more creative than that?

Beware the "Primary Color Trap"

Paint is such a great way to do dynamic design. It's cheap and easy to change. But the colors you choose send less-than-subtle messages to your primary customers ... the kids.

We want our ministries to be colorful and kid-friendly, so we often revert to the weariest of color clichés: primary colors. But painting everything in shades of red, blue, and yellow sends a vivid message to the older kids of your ministry: *this place is for babies.*

for church

HELP! I'M STUCK IN THE PRIMARY COLORS!

How do you create a colorful ministry without making it look like you picked your palette from Rainbow Brite's wardrobe? By remembering that cool flows downhill. Choose trendy colors that have slightly older appeal, and you'll entice your entire audience, oldest kids included.

Want to know how I keep tabs on current colors? I go to Old Navy. This store has got a well-practiced palette when it comes to trend-setting hues. At the time I'm writing this book, their print materials, credit-card applications, and in-store displays make liberal use of turquoise, lime green, and orange. Even my Old Navy credit card reflects these trendy tints. From my experience, when the vogue shifts to a new set of shades, this teen-targeted clothing emporium is the first to know. For me, this store is my barometer for fashionable colors.

Most hot teen colors make fabulous Sunday school shades because they're trendy and forward thinking, but still very bright, colorful, and kid-friendly. Every fifth grader will feel right at home, but you're also creating a sassy and stimulating environment to delight the kindergarten crew.

A note about murals: A common choice for ministry walls, I know. Yet, like primary colors, they send that subtle message ... *"this place is for preschoolers"* ... leaving a less-than-satisfying taste in the mouths of the ministry tweens.

So if you are committed to murals, think about limiting them to your youngest areas. Below five years old. Anywhere else, and prepare to have them silently scorned by the older boys.

SACRE LE BLEU! A MASTERPIECE OF COLOUR HOW DID YOU DO IT?

OLD NAVY PALETTE, BUT OF COURSE.

\$\$ 190,000,000,000

Touch on Texture

Paint and Styrofoam. These are the decor supplies with which children's ministry folks are well-versed.

Signs.

Mangers.

Arks.

Whales.

You name it, we've painted it on a wall or made it out of Styrofoam.

But here's a design principle worth putting your hands on: think texture. Let's touch on a few new materials and approaches that can give your decor a whole new feel.

Metal. This silver stuff immediately gives any decor a slightly industrial look and an edgy air. This is great for older teaching rooms. But don't think you have to wallpaper the room in deck-plating. Using metal as accent pieces—letters on signs, whimsical shapes, metal trusses to frame a staging area—creates heavy duty impact that can work well in any K–5 teaching space. Metal comes in all styles and textures—steel plating with cross-hatch textures, metal mesh, polished aluminum, copper—so there are lots of possibilities.

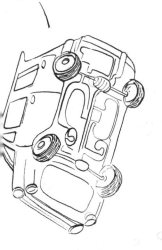

I FIND METAL VERY "ATTRACTIVE"!

METAL MAGNET

Cutting heavy-duty sheet metal into shapes or letters requires a welder or someone with a plasma cutter (check around the church ... you might be surprised to find that you have a metal maniac right under your nose). But there are lots of low-grade options right in the hardware store that can be managed with a good pair of tin snips. Try cutting sign letters out of the metal mesh strips that are used to cover gutters. Or use metal framing studs (these are often used nowadays instead of wooden studs in commercial buildings ... they are inexpensive and can be found in any home improvement store) to build a three-dimensional structure like a phone booth or snack hut.

Fur. It comes in all colors and textures ... animal print, hot pink shag; if you can dream it, you can buy the fuzzy stuff. Robbie Rotten, the villain in Nick Jr.'s *Lazytown*, can often be seen reclining in a funky orange fur chair. The wooly work of art gives his lair the perfect touch, using texture.

You can use fur as furniture covering and carpets, but you can also put the fluffy fabric to more unorthodox uses. Next time you create large wooden letters for a sign, try upholstering them in fur. A staple gun is all you need. You'll create an eye-catching sign that every kid longs to run their fingers over.

Fabric. Known as "soft goods" in the world of theater, fabric is a favorite of stage designers who know how fabulous a few yards of it looks when lights hit it. Hang it from the ceiling in several long columns as a backdrop. Swoop it above the kids with fishing line as fun and free-form overhead art.

With endless textures and designs, from silky to sparkly, patterned to plain, fabric has endless applications in creating breathtaking designs.

Avoid busy patterns or bolts of fabric with little teeny details on them, unless the print gives the flavor you're looking for, like an African print, for example. Instead, opt for larger prints, or textured fabrics with simple patterns. Remember, in most cases the fabric serves as a backdrop, and the purpose of a backdrop is to create a striking background for whatever is in front of it, not to be the featured event itself.

Also, don't be thrown by prices. Some fabrics are very expensive, but by shopping sales, scouring discontinued or remnant tables, or scoping out warehouse fabric supply houses, you can save big bucks while creating an impressive impact.

Beaded curtains. Retro fads aside, these things are just fun to walk through. Drape them over the doorways to your teaching room, for a kid-entrance that jingle-jangle-jingles.

Letters that leap off the wall. Displays in stores (check out the displays in Target near the kid's clothes) often use spacers to make the letters and graphics appear to leap off the background. When making signs, instead of just painting letters onto a background, cut three-dimensional letters out of wood or MDF (medium density fiberboard, a cheap material sold by the sheet, like plywood). Then add a small, one-inch-thick block of wood or Styrofoam behind the letters before mounting them to the background. You can also use washers as spacers, stacking them as high or low as you want, and driving screws from the back of the sign, through the stack of washers, into wooden letters. This creates a drop-shadow behind the letters and adds layers that make your letters really pop off the sign.

➤ *Plexiglas.* An oft overlooked material, Plexiglas looks great as a sign material. It's just as cheap as the poster-grade foam board most of us use for signs, especially if you buy it in larger sheets (check Home Depot or any glass supply store), and can be easily cut with a band saw. Not savvy on saws? Check with a woodworker in the church. Chances are good that they've got a band saw and might be willing to send a few sheets of Plexiglas across the blade for you.

You can paint on Plexiglas, and cutting it into freeform shapes allows you to create quirky, one-of-a-kind signage that has a cool ultramodern look. You can also attach wooden or foam letters onto Plexiglas with a dab of silicone or hot glue, and it can be drilled into for attaching hanging cords or mounting metal letters or shapes into it.

Looking for a cool framing idea for a kid-friendly artwork? Mount a picture on the wall (or paint an image, like a Bible character, directly onto the wall, covering about a two-foot square area). Then mount a three-foot square piece of half-inch Plexiglas on the wall in front of the image, spacing it out from the wall by about six inches using washers (just like with the letters, above). The result frames the picture in an eye-popping way. For

WALL

PICTURE

PLEXIGLASS

STACKS OF WASHERS OR PVC PIPE

WASHERS

SCREWS

MOSES

an extra touch, round the corners of the Plexiglas on the band saw before mounting it, and paint the Bible character's name or a verse directly onto the Plexiglas toward the bottom. This gives you a double-layered effect, since the text seems to float over the image it frames.

Repeat Performance

While browsing at a discount store one day, you find these funky round paper lanterns (IKEA or Target carries stuff like this). Made from white rice paper and about one foot in diameter, they have that perfect coffee-house look, ideal for the fourth- and fifth-grade decor. And at $1 apiece, the price is right. But one lantern is going to get no notice in your teaching room. Splash-factor? Zero. Visual punch? Pitiful.

Want immediate impact? Then just repeat yourself.

Instead of buying just one, get 100 of those groovy little lanterns. Spray-paint them in shades from your design palette. One third of them in lime green; one third in turquoise; one third ... orange. Mix them up and hang them from the ceiling throughout the entire teaching room, at various heights overhead. Instant wow. Visual pizzazz galore. And you didn't break the bank.

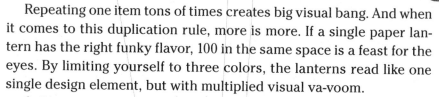

Repeating one item tons of times creates big visual bang. And when it comes to this duplication rule, more is more. If a single paper lantern has the right funky flavor, 100 in the same space is a feast for the eyes. By limiting yourself to three colors, the lanterns read like one single design element, but with multiplied visual va-voom.

Ceilings are a great place to put this repetition principle into practice.

Need a cool overhead feel for a fiesta? I'm thinking piñata! But don't stop with one. In any good-sized teaching room, a single piñata is going to look lonelier than a leftover burrito at an all-you-can-eat buffet. But hang 15 or 20 piñatas overhead, in all shapes and sizes, and you've got Southwest style worth celebrating. I can buy primo piñatas at my local Hispanic grocery for under $12 apiece. Tons of online sources are available too.

While you're repeating yourself, think of out-of-the-ordinary items. Cruise over to a local salvage yard or junkyard and scrounge 20 old bicycles. Spray-paint each one a different color (tires and all) and suspend them from the ceiling at various angles. Talk about dude-friendly design!

Picking cheap items to repeat creates impressive impact without blowing your budget.

How about a beaded-curtain-style backdrop created from 500 blank CDs strung together with fishing line?

Total cost: maybe $100.

Or 50 thrift-store suitcases painted hip colors and stacked all over the stage?

NICE PIÑATAS

Total cost: Ransack the right thrift stores, and you can score old suitcases for a buck or two apiece.

Or old tires (or even hubcaps) spray-painted and mounted in vertical rows from floor to ceiling along the whole back wall.

Total cost: Zip. Nada. Bupkiss. In fact, your local auto repair place might pay you to haul their old tires away.

Being thrilled to repeat yourself, for the first time ever? Well, you can't put a price on that.

TIPS FOR INCORPORATING TECH

When should I add tech into my teaching programs?

What technical elements should I add first?

Do I even need tech?

These are the kinds of questions that light up when we start talking about lights, video, and sound equipment.

Many children's ministries are feeling growth pangs as their churches move from a small church to a medium-sized ministry. Maybe, instead of the 30 kids, your numbers have spiked up to 80 per weekend, and you don't know how to compensate. Tech can help take the message all the way to the back wall, regardless of room size.

If you're already using tech with success, then this may feel rudimentary. Feel free to pass *GO*, collect your $200 ... all that. But if you're looking for some guiding light on adding voltage to tech-free teaching, here's a primer.

Lighting

If your kids have a general restlessness, or you're teaching large amounts of kids in one space (like, over 50), or if you're in a room that's way too big or full of distraction (like a gym), some simple lighting is the tech tool custom-designed to brighten up life for you. No single tech element has the power to focus your audience's attention like lighting.

Try this experiment. This weekend, turn off those glaring florescent overhead lights that typically illuminate the whole room while you're teaching. Instead, bring a small floor lamp up on stage to light the teaching space. You'll be amazed at the power even this small adjustment has to refocus kids' attention during the teaching.

When considering adding technical elements to a tech-challenged teaching space, lighting is first on my list.

When those overhead florescent lights are on, attention is diffused. You want the kids to give you their attention, but your lighting sends a different message. As a kid, every other visual thing in the room (the pictures on the wall, the friend sitting next to me, the ponytail of the girl sitting in front of me that's too tempting not to yank) is competing for my attention.

But when the room is darkened and the teaching space is lit, attention is powerfully refocused frontward. Talking suddenly feels taboo. Your presence commands the space because you and your teaching space are the only things lit.

So let's illuminate some lighting options. While elaborate theater lighting, faders, and lighting boards are always beautiful things, here are some very simple first steps that can lead to lighting success.

Track lighting. Basic track lighting is a great inexpensive way to dip your toes into the lighting pool. Install one or two long tracks on the ceiling in front of the teaching space. This gives you the option of adding extra lights as you go. Once the track is up, the lights themselves can be as cheap as $10 apiece to add more lighting along the way. These days there are also funky tension-line lights that work in the same way. You can check these options out at places like Home Depot. IKEA also has great inexpensive options.

Separate control. Bring in an electrician who can do some rewiring. You'll want to have lighting tracks wired in separately to a new switch or control, so they don't run on the same circuit as the rest of the overhead florescent stuff. If you have two

tracks put in, have each one wired to a separate wall switch, for even more control. Hiring an electrician is the most expensive part of the operation, but well worth it. The lights do you no good if you can't control them separate from the room lights. You might be able to find an electrician who attends the church who would do the work for free.

Switch to a dimmer. For an extra buck and a half, have your electrician put in a dimmer switch. This enables you to fade the lights up and down, versus just a light-on/light-off effect. This makes for slick transitions to videos and sweet fade-outs between the teaching and the puppet sketch.

DID YOU HEAR ABOUT PHILLIP? THEY PUT HIM ON A DIMMER!

OH MY!

Tech toys. While you're at it, consider having a few fun-effect lights put in. Spinning color wheels, disco balls, spinning police lights ... all these can bring great energy to worship times and give you creative options for teaching times. You can often find this stuff at DJ supply places ... scope out the back of the book for additional sources (page 319).

When you're ready to upgrade to other options, theater lights are for you. Many theater-lighting places offer consultation to help determine what will set you up to score without blowing the budget. Again, check the appendix for some sources (page 319).

Video

Still using a regular television for videos, even though you've moved into a bigger space?

Feel like you're losing the back half of the room every time you drop a DVD into the program?

Are the worship words so small on the screen that you can't read them, even with your new glasses?

It may be time to upgrade to wide-screen projection for video support.

The ability to use video for PowerPoint Bible verses, song slides, or DVD clips is a big gun in your creative teaching arsenal, one well worth investing in. But don't worry ... wide-screen video projection doesn't have to cost an arm and a leg.

Many churches start off with a freestanding video projection unit (as opposed to a ceiling-mounted model). You can find them these days for under $1,000, with this figure continuing to plummet as the technology gets cheaper. Load it onto a wheeled cart, and put a DVD player and a VCR on the shelf underneath. You can even plug your laptop into the mix to pipe in your PowerPoint slides. Plug your power strip into an outlet, use a blank wall for a screen, and *Lights Out!* You've got a mobile movie theater.

But if you're already running a setup like this, it may be time to give the nod to a ceiling-mounted version. Getting cheaper by the day, a built-in projection unit takes all the awkwardness out of the cart-mounted model. No more dragging wires to trip over, no more Sunday morning setup, no more search and rescue for the vid cart because the high school ministry heisted it ... a ceiling-mounted model gives you flip-the-switch convenience and control.

For projecting that image ... wall-mounted side screens are common options, but those puppies can be pricey. For the fiscally minded, I'm a fan of pull-down style projection screens like we used to watch filmstrips on in biology class. Put one dead-center on the wall behind your teaching stage, and yank it into place when you want to roll tape.

One of these days, that awkward AV cart with the 47-inch TV bungee-corded to the top is going to tip over and flatten you like a pancake. Those monsters weigh about as much as a fridge. Think about making the switch to wide-screen projection. It'll bring a whole new level of media-minded possibilities to your teaching lesson.

And maybe even save you from a serious squashing.

OH YEAH SURE

IS IT SAFE?

DON'T BECOME A PANCAKE!

Sound

CD players, microphones, amplification systems ... all of this sound technology becomes increasingly important as a ministry grows in size. Sure, it was no problem making yourself heard in the back room of the basement with 20 kids, but now that you're meeting in the gym and the kids are pushing maximum capacity, your ability to teach effectively and powerfully can be majorly enhanced by a little technology.

Sounds expensive, I know. But don't fret yet. It doesn't all have to happen at once. Here are some thoughts to help you prioritize.

Scott Reisdorf at The Chapel in North Canton, Ohio, says that layering in sound equipment a little at a time was absolutely critical to their tech success.

"Prioritizing was so important," Scott says. "We got some great advice from within the congregation after we found out that several people in the church actually install sound equipment for a living."

That's insight worth putting on the loudspeaker. Before moving forward, put your ear to the ground and find out what experts exist within your midst. Or maybe there are sound gurus or electricians in the community who have a soft spot for the church. Some expert advice on the front end can save serious time and money.

So, when it comes to sound equipment, what should you add first?

CD players are at the top of my list for their ability to add snap, crackle, and pop to your teaching programs. Playing worship tracks, adding music soundtracks or sound effects to storytelling ... for any of this a CD player is a must. And while you're at it, put in two. By cheaply adding two or three CD players, instead of one, you can easily tighten up sound cues and upgrade excellence. Want to play dramatic music for the story of Peter denying Jesus and also layer in the rooster crowing after Peter disses Jesus that third time? Two CD players make it possible.

TWO CDS ARE BETTER THAN ONE! — AGREED.

Simple boom boxes or an iPod hooked up to speakers can get the job done, but if your growth curve is on the move, you need to think "amplification" next.

"We were lucky to inherit a room with a built-in speaker system," says Scott Reisdorf. "But you can also buy stand-alone amplifiers at any guitar center for about $400. That's what I would have used if we hadn't been blessed with the built-in stuff."

Scott's offering up sound advice. While a built-in sound system may make your mouth water, purchasing stand-alone amps can still open new channels of communication for teachers, who will suddenly have the loudest voice in the room without getting laryngitis in the process. You can wire a single microphone into the amp and run your CD player to it as well. It keeps the sound coming from the front, where you want it, and with long enough cables or extension wires, you can have a separate person run the CD player from the back of the room. This may be a great intermediate step for now, if dreams of built-in sound equipment need to stay temporarily on hold.

"Once we had amplification happening, things were really enhanced," Scott says. "The kids were pumped, worship times rocked. But we discovered that our room was never designed with acoustics in mind."

Sound familiar? Those of us who are basement dwellers often try to make miracles happen in rooms that were designed for much less inspired pursuits.

"The room echoed like a cave. The kids were really having a hard time making out the words. So we had an acoustical engineer come in. He quoted us $15,000 to add acoustic panels to the room and change everything out. But we came up with our own solution. For a measly $1,500, we spent a weekend building carpet-covered acoustic panels. We built frames out of simple two-by-twos and coated them with cheap indoor/outdoor carpeting using staple guns. We hung these all over the walls in a cool geometric pattern." (Check your fire codes before going carpet-crazy ... some areas require that panels like this be fireproof as well as soundproof.)

It may not have been "acoustically engineered," but at one-tenth the cost, Scott's team did the job.

"It completely deadened the sound. The result was great. The echo was gone. You could hear worship and teaching and movie clips so much more clearly."

Live bands and wireless mikes aren't necessarily the formula for sound success. While these bells and whistles can certainly help a lesson sing, it's important to remember that they are tools to support a dynamic teacher. A gifted teacher communicating the Bible with skill and power is always the main attraction. So assess the room you have to work with, and add what you think will best enhance your lessons for now.

"These days we use wireless mikes, live bands, and a nicely equipped sound board," Scott says. "But it took over six years to get there. It's definitely a process."

So continue to dream big. After all, a fresh new untouched budget, full of technological possibilities, is less than a year away.

PART THREE

Power
Tools
of

CREATIVITY

Part Three Introduction

A loaded up tool belt. Stocked to the hilt. That's what a master carpenter needs to build with excellence. I'm no master carpenter, but I know you can't use a hammer for everything. I admit I once attempted to use a hammer to remove a stripped screw from a door. And to remove a broken light bulb. And to cut down a tree (don't ask … it's not a pretty picture). Bottom line: regardless of how much technique you have, one tool is simply not sufficient. 'Nuff said.

The same principle applies when it comes to transformational teaching. I want my creative tool belt to be jam-packed with possibilities … chockfull of tools I can pull out and use, no matter what Bible story I face … overflowing with creative methods that bring great variety to lessons, the kind of variety kids really respond to.

You'll see that this section is a little different than the rest of the book, I hope you'll find it a bit handbooky … a reference guide. Feel free to bend these pages a-plenty when planning your upcoming lessons, or during rehearsal when you're looking for that next new way to tell a Bible story.

Regardless of how you use it, you'll see that the following pages are packed with 20 different tried-and-true methods for teaching the Bible creatively. I've shop tested them all. These are tools for your creative tool belt. These are tools that could be unleashed on any Bible story. These are tools to bring the Bible to life with power and creativity in a way that mesmerizes and transforms kids.

So put on your safety glasses. When you rev these creative tools into high gear on your Bible lessons, sparks are gonna fly.

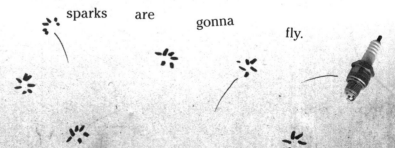

208

CHAPTER 12

20 WAYS TO TEACH THE BIBLE CREATIVELY

Method 1:

Audience Participation 1:
HAND-PICKED PARTICIPANTS

No matter what limitations you face—limited budget, limited time, limited creativity—you always have one thing at your disposal ... the kids in the room. So bring them up on stage.

It Works Like This

Ask for volunteers to help you tell the story. You'll usually get a huge response (everyone wants to come up and help). Pick out as many as you need. Bring them up and give them *simple* instructions. Tell the story. Cue them when they need to do their part, but stay in control of the lesson throughout.

It's always unexpected. But almost always a winner.

It Looks Like This

Example: David and Goliath

I pick 14 kids to come up on stage. I put six on one side of the stage and give each one a plastic sword. The Philistines. My instructions to them: "When I get to your part of the story, I'll point to you and say, 'PHILISTINES.' When I do that, I need you to rattle your swords and sing (I demonstrate, complete with air-guitar solo), 'We ... are the champions ... my friend!'" (Unfamiliar? Just pick up *Queen's Greatest Hits* or go to a soccer game sometime. You'll be in the loop.)

I put six more kids on the other side of the stage and give each a plastic sword. The Israelites. Instructions: "When I get to your part of the story, I'll point to you and say, 'ISRAELITES.' When I do that, you rattle your swords kind of halfheartedly (you're losing the battle, after all) and say 'Oh, ma-a-a-a-a-n!'"

I have one kid stand on a chair. I put a really long robe on him (long enough to cover the chair) so he looks huge. Goofy helmet on his head. Mop (as a spear) in his hand. Instant Goliath. His instructions: "When I point to you and say, 'GOLIATH!', give me your biggest, evil-est, *MWAA-HA-HA-HA*-est villain laugh."

My last remaining kid, I deck out in shepherd headgear, a crook, and a strap sling. His instructions: "Just follow my lead."

Now, the pieces are in place for great storytelling. Philistines sing. Israelites sulk. Goliath laughs. David whoops up. Goliath hams up the death scene. The story gets taught in an incredibly memorable way. Everyone goes home happy.

Example: The Last Supper

The stage is set with a huge table and 13 chairs. I have an unsliced loaf of bread, a goblet, and a pitcher of grape juice. I pick 12 kids (both boys and girls) to come up and join me as the disciples. This time, the kids have no real instructions. They are little more than living props as I storytell through the night of The Last Supper, slipping in and out of being the storyteller and *becoming* Jesus. When the bread part comes, I break it and pass it. The 12 eat. The power is palpable. When the cup part comes, I pour it and pass it, and all 12 take a sip (it's just 13 of us, so I risk the cootie-factor in favor of bringing this amazing story to life).

No instructions. No lines for the kids to say. Almost no props. Sounds almost too easy. The key is really *becoming* Jesus at the key moments, addressing the 12 directly at certain moments. The kids sense the weight of this incredibly significant moment in Jesus' life, and become part of it in a unique way.

211

MWAAAAAA-HAAA-HAAAAAAA-HAAAAAAAA

AAAAAH!

Helpful Little Hints

○ ***Keep the instructions easy.*** This method requires no rehearsal ... for the kids, that is. Because of that, keep your instructions to the kids simple. Don't expect them to execute organized or well-timed cues. Not only will it fall apart, the time it takes to give them the instructions bogs down the entire lesson. It should take no longer than 30 seconds to tell the Philistines what to say, when to say it, and to practice it once. Oh, and on that topic ... just because this requires no preparation for the kids, doesn't mean we should be winging it too. We need to be well prepared and memorized so we are confident when things take unexpected turns, as they so often do when you have 14 kids on stage with you.

○ ***Stay in the driver's seat.*** While it may seem like the kids are the main attraction in this method, the real power comes from gifted storytelling. You need to stay in charge and not let the Philistines get drawn into a Jedi light saber battle with their swords at your most crucial moment. Some tangible ways to stay in control:

● *Preparation.* When you are prepared, you are confident.

● *Proximity.* When David starts hamming it up, move closer to him while you tell the story.

HERE ARE SOME SIMPLE INSTRUCTIONS:

STAY

SIT

EAT

DRINK

YELL

LAUGH

SLEEP

SNORE

BRING ME THE REMOTE

I'll even put my hand on his shoulder as a subtle signal: "I'm driving buddy, back off a bit."

- *Be careful who you pick.* A group of fifth-grade boys with swords in their hands is a recipe for a full-scale battle sequence. So I always mix up my group of Philistines. I pick some younger kids or some girls (let's just admit it, they're more well behaved). Even a leader ... the leader's presence just seems to anchor the group and help maintain focus.

○ **Be trustworthy.** One of the reasons every hand shoots up whenever I ask for volunteers is that I've proven myself trustworthy with my kids. They know I'm not going to embarrass them, humiliate them, or make them do anything cheesy or goofy. This is a huge ingredient in the recipe for success with this method—kids must know they are safe being on stage with you. Never break that trust.

Method 2:

Audience Participation 2:
INVOLVING THE WHOLE ROOM

There's another way to play the audience-participation game that involves every kid in the room. Leading an entire mob of kids through an orchestrated experience ... dictating what they say, where they move, when they stop ... it can create some pretty powerful Bible teaching.

Just don't let all that power go to your head.

It Works Like This

Sometimes it means breaking the crowd into groups ... "This half of the room is the Philistines and this half of the room is the Israelites" ... like that. In this arrangement, you can assign each group things to say, just like the first style of audience participation ... only en masse.

But other times it works best if you treat the whole gang as one

group. Have them all be the Israelite army marching around Jericho. Have them all sit around the table at the Last Supper. Have them all create the storm that Jesus calms. How you sort them depends on the story you're trying to teach, the number of kids in the room, and your own personal teaching preference.

It Looks Like This

Example: Jesus and the Storm

The story of Jesus calming the storm is totally awesome. But it sometimes loses something in the telling. It's hard to truly imagine that incredible storm coming to a screeching halt ... unless you re-create it.

For this one, I bring three kids up on stage to be my disciples. I put them in my boat (which is just three chairs turned backwards) and they take over rowing duty as I tell the story. So far, it sounds a lot like the first version of audience participation, right?

Just wait.

When I get to the part where the rain begins, I direct the audience at key sections of the story to provide the sound effects. They are instructed to rub their hands together (for light rain), continually snap (for plip-plopping raindrops), repeatedly slap their legs (when the storm kicks into high gear), and boom like thunder. A virtual typhoon is created in the room as the kids commit 110 percent to their part of the storm, and it's always a moment like no other when I (as Jesus) say, "Peace, be still," and everything comes to a halt. At that point, the scripted lesson says, "And the disciples were amazed ..."

And, truth be told, so are the kids.

Example: The Walls of Jericho

A pile of old cardboard boxes is stacked in the middle of the room, floor to ceiling, when the kids arrive in the room. Unknown to the kids, there's a helper hiding in the heap, ready to trigger a cardboard avalanche of boxes at the right moment. But not yet.

The helper climbed in there and the boxes were built around him before the kids came in. Yep, he has to hide in there for a while.

Dressed in a military uniform, the teacher, as Joshua, informs the kids that they are the Israelite army and their instructions from God are to destroy the city of Jericho. But upon further inspection, he reveals to the kids that God's instructions are a bit odd.

So, led by Joshua, the kids march around the cardboard city one time. Sleepy lullaby music signals nightfall on day one, and they all lay down on the ground to sleep. But the blaring of reveille on a bugle awakens the army for day two, and again, they march. They repeat this cycle seven times. A military march blasts on the CD player as they march. Day three. Day four. Day five. Finally, day seven arrives. Joshua gives them their day seven instructions ... they are to march around the city seven times this time, and when the trumpets blast, they are to yell. And so, the whole pint-sized army marches around the cardboard Jericho, as Joshua counts them off. One! Two! Three!... Seven! With eager anticipation, they turn. They face Jericho. The trumpet blasts from the CD player. They yell.

And as eyes widen, a slow shimmer shakes the cardboard citadel and gradually turns violent, collapsing the walls around them!

Victory!

Helpful Little Hints

○ **Make the kids active participants.** Make sure the kids' part in the proceedings remains active. If you're telling the story of the lost sheep, for example, don't just have them crawl around on all fours baaa-ing the whole time. Not unless you're a fan of total anarchy. Keep their role specific and ongoing. Make them an army that has to carry out a series of instructions. Let them be creators of a storm that gradually builds rather than setting them on "hurricane" mode for five minutes straight. By keeping them active, you keep them on their toes for the unexpected.

○ **Instruct as you go.** Don't give the crowd all their instructions right up front. Fill them in as you fly through the lesson. If they think they've got your formula all figured out from the get-go, they tend to take liberties with it. Since they know what's coming, thunder becomes fart noises and yelling at the walls becomes a contest between boys to see who has the guts to "accidentally" kick over the city walls. By keeping them in the dark, you keep them tuned in. Their ears remain open for the next instruction, waiting for you to reveal the next wrinkle in the plot.

○ **Mix and match.** Use this second style of audience participation in conjunction with the first version ... like in the Jesus-and-the-storm example. This gives you the chance to incorporate both leading characters and crowd scenes. For example, you can break the whole mob into Israelites and Philistines to incorporate the entire room but also bring up on stage a specific David and Goliath who will play a more featured part.

baaa

○ **Make creative use of space.** Use the room in a unexpected way. If you break the room into Israelites and Philistines, then split the kids at the middle line and bring your David and Goliath between the two. Suddenly, the whole scene is playing out in the round, which adds unexpectedness and immerses the kids right into the middle of the scene. Check out Method 16 (Around the Room, page 274) for more ideas on this.

baaa

baaa

Method 3:

Art Attack

I've seen chalk talks and storytelling with art before, but some friends of mine—Dave Huber and Holly Laurent—came up with a simplified version that was immediately accessible and current all in one shot. No good at drawing? No problem. This method is a work of art for even the most paintbrush-challenged.

It Works Like This

The basic premise is to identify key visual parts of the story and paint them as you go. Stick figures are fine. Simple is fine—in fact, it's best. This isn't a fine art contest; this is a fun and sometimes silly way of visualizing the story.

The key for success here is setup. You need to know exactly what you're going to paint, and in what order. Ideally, make it people and places (things you can see), but you can add action by using dashed arrows or movement lines (things like quivering lines around a stick figure to represent someone who's scared). Feel free to add clarity by using words to label things (like places). Also, set up your supplies in advance. A large canvas to draw on, with a long table to hold the paints and brushes is perfect. And use lots of colors. Have the paint (tempera works great) already squirted out on little paper plates, with a brush for each color ready to go. This keeps things moving forward as you tell the story; you don't want to get bogged down in the supplies.

KER-SPLAT!

baa.

It Looks Like This

Example: Joshua and Caleb

This is the Dave and Holly original. When I get to each part of the story, I paint that element, storytelling through it. I try to avoid stopping completely to paint, but rather, paint and talk simultaneously. On the next two pages you'll see the final picture when I'm done, along with the order in which I paint each thing.

Example: Saul Chasing David — The Tepee Art Attack

My team once created a 3-D version of the Art Attack by building a tepee. Three sticks in the middle (tied at the top) with butcher paper (or even white fabric, like muslin) wrapped around it to form a tepee. We painted right onto the tepee. For the story of Saul hunting down David that's found in 1 Samuel 21–23, this was a great method. During some of the story, Saul is hunting David around a mountain, so the tepee itself served as that mountain. We mounted the tepee onto a base with wheels, so we could spin it around like a lazy Susan. This gave us every side to paint on.

While the story at first glance seems to be all action (which means lots of arrows and stick figures) and nothing else visual to paint, we found lots of stuff to paint: a building with the word "Nob" over it for when David flees to the village of Nob, a piece of pizza for when Ahimelech gives David food, a gigantic sword for when Ahimelech gives David Goliath's sword, a stick figure with a mean face for Saul's servant in Nob, and tons of other stuff. The trick is to dig out all those fun or interesting details that bring the story to life.

Helpful Little Hints

○ *Use lots of mediums.* I use several small foam brushes, but don't stop there! Incorporate rollers (you can buy cheap sponge versions at craft stores) to paint those lush rolling hills or desert dunes. Sponge on red paint to create the brick walls of Jericho. Cut colored masking tape into unique shapes for quick, stick-on accents. Think chalk, airbrush, spray paint (beware of the fumes, though), even clay! The combinations are endless.

○ *Make hidden messages.* One of the coolest parts of the Joshua and Caleb story is when the teacher reveals that the verse is hidden right in the pictures they've drawn. It's Joshua 1:9: "Be (the bee) strong (the muscle guy from Canaan) and courageous (that's Joshua and Caleb) for (the 4 from 40) the Lord your God

("God" at the top) will be (again, the bee) with you wherever (the arrows going back and forth to Canaan) you go." By planning the pictures well, you could do this with any verse for any story. It's a great "aha!" moment at the end as you drive the Bible truth home.

○ **Think big.** Avoid using a teeny white board or flip chart for this. I know that's easiest, but the scale is too small and it doesn't have the same effect. So where do you get a mammoth canvas? You *make* one using butcher paper and two eight-foot tables (the kind with folding legs that you have in your church).

Set up one table normally. Put the other table on top of it, on its side (so the tabletop is facing the audience). Run a roll of butcher paper or white paper along the upright tabletop (it might take two lengths to cover the whole area), and tape it in place. Instant eight-foot canvas! I usually clamp the legs of the top table to the tabletop of the bottom one (using C-clamps or spring clamps) so it doesn't slide off. I also leave about a one foot space on my bottom tabletop, right in front of my new "canvas," so I can put my paints and brushes within easy reach.

223

○ *Team teach.* This is a great time to incorporate a new teacher or apprentice into your teaching, because this style works great with two teachers. Since there's drawing time involved, one teacher can continue to move the story along while the other paints. It also allows for fun banter and humor between the teachers that can be developed at rehearsal.

○ # Method 4:

One-Man Show

No matter how diverse our ministries may be, we all share one common struggle. Shortage of gifted teachers. Maybe you're the exception to that rule, in which case the rest of us have all planned a recruitment road trip to your church this weekend. See you Sunday.

But for the rest of us, there's a great creative teaching method that maximizes our minimal numbers in a powerful way to bring a story to life. The One-Man Show.

It Works Like This

One teacher.

A coatrack or simple dressing screen.

Fill that coatrack with at least one prop (hats, beards, scarves) for every character in your Bible story.

Then tell the story and become all the characters along the way, changing props as you become each new character. Use character voices and dialects throughout to keep the characters distinct, and talk *as* the characters versus narrating *about* them whenever possible.

It Looks Like This

Example: David and Goliath

A great story for this method. A coatrack with a little kid hat for David, warrior helmet and spear for Goliath, old man beard for Jessie, and army helmet and riding crop for King Saul. Fun characterizations bring everything to life. I do Jesse with a thick Jewish accent (Miracle Max out of *The Princess Bride*), a little Schwarzenegger for Goliath, and King Saul becomes a John Wayne-style drill sergeant.

Example: The Old Testament Rewind

This is taking this tool to the nth degree. Four actors tell the entire story of the Old Testament, running around and playing all (okay, most) of the characters. While it's a prop nightmare and has enough memorization to leave you curled up in the fetal position for a week afterward, this extreme approach is anything but boring. Because of all the quick changes, we've graduated up from a coatrack to a full-blown folding screen, and I usually keep several hinge-lidded boxes behind the screen, both for tucking away props and standing on when I want to pop over the top of the screen rather than coming all the way around. The result? Afterward, most of the fifth graders in the room can remember a detailed chronology of the entire Old Testament. Cold.

P.S. While this is just an example of what's possible, if you ever want to do the Old Testament Rewind in its script form, the script is available at *www.promiselandonline.com.*

It's requires four actors and runs about 25 minutes.

HEE HEE HOO HOO HA HA HEE HEE HOO HOO HA HA HEE HEE

Helpful Little Hints

○ *Embrace your inner idiot.* Half the fun for the kids is watching the storyteller struggle to "become" each new character. A lot of the power of the Old Testament Rewind is in this manic and silly pace. The doctrine is sound; the theology is accurate. But let's face it, to a kid there's nothing quite like watching a grown man race around like a maniac desperately trying to get his Moses beard off so he can become Joshua three seconds later.

○ *Take your time.* While some sense of mania is a necessary component to this method, a lot of it is manufactured. Faked. Put on. Control is the real key. Don't let the story spiral into true hysteria and start dragging you through the lesson like a runaway Great Dane on a leash. Set the controls at "energized" and don't let the switch slip up to "runaway train." There's nothing funny about watching real panic set in.

○ *Easy on, easy off.* Pick props that offer maximum fun factor with minimum chance of a wardrobe traffic jam. Hats work great. Beards? Perfect, the cheap ones with the elastic string being ideal. Handheld things like spears and swords? Excellent. Vests? Pretty good. Shirts and things that go over the head are out. And goofy shoes? Well, now you're just being silly.

○ *Think unusual.* When picking your props, go out of your way to find off-the-wall choices. A simple baseball cap for David may be easiest for you to scrounge up around the house, but it's just not as effective as a beanie with a little propeller on top. Visit a well-stocked costume shop, especially around Halloween, to stock up on inexpensive but unusual accessories. And when you can, splurge on those items you know will get used a lot. I've never regretted spending 45 bucks on a really cool Pharaoh headdress. Everyone in the church comes looking for it when a Moses lesson rolls around.

Method 5:

Visual Props

We've all used this one before. There's no doubt that just holding something in your hand for the kids to look at helps settle the kids down (not to mention your nerves). But what if we took this tool a step further? By stringing together a series of purposefully picked props, we draw kids into the story like a trail of bread crumbs and provide easy-to-remember landmarks along the way.

It Works Like This

Break the story or biblical concept into five or six sections. Then find a unique or visually interesting prop to attach to each section:

- A broken ruler for when Adam and Eve break the rules in the garden

- Swimming flippers for the crossing of the Jordan River

- Chocolate-dipped grasshoppers to introduce John the Baptist (hey, honey and locusts ... chocolate and grasshoppers ... close enough).

Then tell the story, creatively revealing the props as you go. For example:

- Line up six stools, each with a prop on it, and cover them with handkerchiefs. Tell the story, uncovering each prop along the way.

- Pack all the props into a suitcase. Then unpack the story.

- Gift wrap each prop in a separate box. Unwrap things as you go.

It Looks Like This

Example: The 12 Unstoppable Disciples

The story of Jesus and his unstoppable mission is perfect for a spy approach. In a unit called *Mission Unstoppable*, a metal briefcase is packed with 12 unique props, one to represent each disciple. As the teacher carries out his mission of introducing the kids to Jesus' unstoppable team of 12 ... well, let's face it ... 12 dudes is a lot to remember. The props provide memory hooks to help kids stay on track ... a big question mark symbolizes Thomas, a pair of fishing poles stand for Peter and Andrew, and Matthew the tax collector (also known as Levi) ... what else? A pair of jeans. Levis, of course.

Example: Run Through the Bible

Kids are often used to dealing with information in a fairly linear, sequential way. So understanding the sequence of the Bible, which, in sections, isn't even in chronological order, can really throw them a curve ball and leave them scratching their aching noggins. For many years, my friend Bob Gustafson knocked this curve ball out of the park by teaching a five-week unit called *Run Through the Bible*. Breaking the Bible into 24 sections, and circling the room with 24 different props on rows of stools (a globe for creation, a broken ruler for the first sin, and so on), he gave kids a clear and linear lowdown on the layout of the Good Book.

Helpful Little Hints

O *Holey briefcase!* You can certainly just have your props lined up on stools like Bob did in *Run Through the Bible,* but anytime you can add a creative or unusual method of revealing the props, you layer intrigue into the lesson. For example, in "Mission Unstoppable," use a metal briefcase placed on a skirted card table. The props are pre-stashed under the table, but when you "reach into" the open briefcase, you actually make a grab under the table. This allows you to seemingly pull huge items out of the briefcase ... like a fishing pole, or a

RULER

glub
glub

gigantic question mark made out of a pool noodle ... the kind of stuff that should never be able to fit in the briefcase. Kids are amazed to see these unexpected items come out of the little silver case.

○ *Out of the ordinary.* Go for out-of-the-ordinary props—things kids don't see everyday. For example, a giant swordfish from a taxidermist's wall. One of those old-timey bicycles with the big front wheel. Whatever. Thrift stores and resale shops are a great place to find the unexpected. Once, while using this method to tell the story of David and Goliath, I used an eight-foot cutout of Michael Jordan to symbolize the big warrior, Goliath. While it certainly would have been easier to just use a plastic sword or something I had readily lying around, this unusual prop created drama. This oversized mystery prop also added intrigue as I went down the line of cloth-covered props, revealing the story bit by bit.

○ *Combo!* Combine the use of visual props with "Motions and Phrases" (Method 13, page 259). This makes a lesson auditory, visual, and kinesthetic all in one fell swoop. Bob did this in his *Run Through the Bible* by attaching phrases to each section and each prop (check out Method 13 for the skinny on these fab phrases). And, by adding a physical motion to each phrase and prop, he brought action and an additional memory handle to the story sequence.

○ *Repeat performance.* Kids love the challenge of going back to the top and trying to remember the story in order. In *Run Through the Bible*, Bob frequently (and literally!) runs back to the top of the sequence and plows through the whole chronology. Sometimes he does it in fast motion, sometimes in slow motion, sometimes with an Arnold Schwarzenegger accent just for fun, but always with the kids joining along. This creates a

high energy, infectious, and unforgettable experience that keeps the fun level high, uses repetition for reinforcement, and makes the Testaments more tangible.

Method 6:

Special Guest Demonstration

A fresh perspective. A new face. A unique talent. Sometimes that's all it takes to grab kids' attention in an unexpected way and prepare them for your Bible lesson. Enter ... the special guest.

It Works Like This

Your cousin is a real live shepherd. Sheep, pasture, the whole shebang.

Your landlord is a metal sculptor. Who doesn't love a welding torch? Honestly.

A friend of a friend of a friend, you find out, races chopper motorcycles. Vroom vroom.

As you plan lessons, be on the lookout for how you could incorporate these, or some other uniquely talented guest, into the lesson.

Remember, this is a Bible lesson, and Bible content needs to stay front and center. But an interesting special guest can provide an unforgettable on-ramp into dynamic Bible teaching.

That shepherd could set up the story of the lost sheep in a very compelling way.

The metal sculptor could be a unique lead-in about Solomon building the temple.

The motorcycle guy ... well, two out of three ain't bad.

It Looks Like This

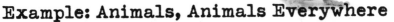

Example: Animals, Animals Everywhere

I once brought in an animal handler as a special guest. She decked out the teaching stage with cages draped in colorful cloths, and one by one revealed a bearded dragon, cockatoo, ferret, and rose-haired tarantula. I was careful to contain her time to about seven minutes of my 25-minute lesson, lest the whole program become animal show-and-tell. Her attention-grabbing demonstration gave me a super springboard into my Bible lesson on creation. Needless to say, I had the full attention of the room, complete with realistic smells to complete the atmosphere. Lining up my animal expert took almost no work ... I put in a few calls to some of the more exotic pet stores in the area and they hooked me up. The animal handler was delighted to do multiple services for free.

Example: Black-Belt Bible Lesson

I once taught a unit called "Running the Race," based on teaching from the books of Hebrews and 1 Timothy about training for godliness. I wanted a dynamic lead-in that played heavily on the training analogy. So I brought in a kung fu master. Obviously, right? Okay, maybe not so obvious.

This guy was good. I would have put this black belt's nunchuck twirling and staff slinging up against Jackie Chan any day. I asked him to prepare a three-minute free-standing demonstration of his skill ... the really flashy stuff. I put on some rockin' music and turned him loose on the stage. Every boy in the room swallowed his gum. This guy had some serious moves … nunchucks, kicks, flips … you name it, he could hi-yah it. After he was done, I did a mini-interview right there in front of the kids. I asked him how he got so good.

His answer: "Practice." We talked about his detailed practice regimen and discovered that a person doesn't just wake up one day with black-belt kung fu skills. It takes practicing every day.

And the same is true with godliness. We must practice godliness. Train for it.

I had my lead-in to unpack 1 Timothy 4:7–8. And every kid was listening.

Helpful Little Hints   HAMSTERS

○ **Prep the guest.** If I had just turned my animal expert loose, who knows what might have come crashing out of her mouth. A mini-lecture in Darwinism, for all I know. Prep your guests. Let them know exactly what you need the kids to hear that will set up the Bible content to win. Let them know they are part of a bigger lesson that needs to drive to a specific point. If that doesn't work for them, then I'm afraid we can't do business together. This isn't a platform for them to spout an agenda — it is an intentional well-planned Bible lesson for the purpose of life transformation.

○ **Use the guest as a starter.** When I bring in a special guest, I almost always put them at the top of the lesson. Here's why: I don't want the last thing kids remember to be "We saw a kung fu guy today!" The kung fu guy is a means to an end, an attention-grabber, an appetizer for better things to come. I want them to walk away with the point the kung fu guy set up … that godliness requires daily training. Training like reading the Bible. Like prayer. Like flexing your obedience muscles in little ways everyday … not lying … not cheating … not stealing. These take-homes are the main course. The kung fu is only there to whet the appetite.

EMPEROR
PENGUIN

MOO

○ ***Don't reach.*** Make sure the guest you bring in really does provide a solid link into the content. Yes, I might bring in a real shepherd to set up the lesson on the lost sheep. There's a strong, clear tie to the content. She can tell us firsthand the lengths she'd go to to find a lost sheep ... maybe even tell a spine-tingling story about a real experience. No reaching required. But I'd probably take a pass on bringing in the drill sergeant to explain the gory principles of war as a setup for my lesson on David and Goliath. While it might grab kids' attention, I'd have to stretch with all the agility of a contortionist to work my way back to the content. Ask yourself the question: Will the content be clearer as a result of this guest?

○ *Method 7:*

THE GAME SHOW

The interactive nature of game shows makes them a sure-fire choice for teaching the Bible creatively. Since game shows often involve some level of audience participation or kid contestants, they are a very kinesthetic way to learn. The challenge is to keep the game targeted toward the content and not let it spiral into a fun-only free-for-all. But if you can overcome this potential trap, your lessons will be winning the grand prize every time.

It Works Like This

Even old-school examples like *The Newlywed Game* or *The Price Is Right* can have a new life as a great game show in your lessons. Keep your eyes peeled for game shows on TV, especially on kid-centric channels like Nickelodeon or the Disney Channel, scoping out formats you can borrow.

Once you ID a game format you like, figure out what role it plays in your lesson. Is it a fun setup to drive toward your main point? Is it a great way of reviewing the story? Is there a way to use a game to actually reveal the story itself? This will help you use it for maximum impact.

It Looks Like This

Example: The God's Hall of Fame Game

Credit for this one goes out to my pal Deanna Armentrout. Taking a new slant on a very old game, she turned *To Tell the Truth* into a dynamic way to review a Bible story and go deeper into a Bible character's life. After hearing the story of Deborah, kids were transitioned into the "God's Hall of Fame Game," where they came face-to-face with ... not one ... not two ... but three, count 'em, three Deborahs. But only one of the guests was the "real" Deborah; the other two were imposters. Decked out in different Bible outfits, but all wearing the same "Deborah" nametag, the special guests fielded questions from four teams of kids in the audience. No guesswork required here ... the kids were given cards with questions to ask, and even the Deborahs had pre-scripted answers. The goal? From what they knew about the story of Deborah, the kids had to determine who was the real Deborah. This game show was so successful, we used it in a six-week series, trying to identify the real deal from the imposters among three Davids, three Esthers, three Gideons, three Jonahs, and three Solomons.

Example: You've Got a Friend in Me

In writing a lesson on salvation, I needed a strong setup to help kids understand the value of having a best friend with them all the time. This ultimately led me into a detailed explanation on how they could enter into a "forever friend" kind of relationship with Jesus. I decided a game show between best friends would do the job nicely.

Borrowing the format from *The Newlyweds Game*, I put three sets of best friends back to back. I asked the three pairs of pals multiple-choice questions about their best friend, and they had to answer what they thought their best friend would say. (They did this by holding up a sign with either A, B, or C on it.) The goal: Be the buddies who know the most about each other.

This simple but fun game is a great reminder of how awesome it is to have a best friend who knows you. But more than that, it's a dynamic lead-in to hear about how Jesus is the best friend of all.

Helpful Little Hints

○ *Grand prizes.* Prizes are a great way to up the ante of excitement and enthusiasm during a game show. When the game involves bringing a few kids up out of the audience, I make sure everyone who has the guts to take the stage walks away with some kind of prize, but I set aside something a little grander for the winner. The more unusual the prize, the better the kid reactions. I've used action figures, glow sticks, a, and lollipops with real bugs imbedded inside. In this day of overweight kids and hyperactivity, I try to stay away from sugar, but for sheer gross-out boy-factor, you can't beat a sucker with a real spider inside it.

○ *Bells and whistles.* Make the experience as interactive as possible by incorporating real props and sound effects. Don't just have contestants raise their hands to answer questions, make it a race to ding in on the bell or blow the kazoo. How about a real digital timer or clock counting down the number of seconds left in the round? And when the end of the round final arrives, blast a CD sound effect as a signal ... a foghorn, a chicken noise, a monkey screech, it doesn't matter. Try playing theme music underneath any question-asking segments. You can find these types of sound effects and game show music CDs near the "soundtracks" section in music stores. But don't stop with official game show CDs. Sometimes you can find CDs that have TV show themes, sports team themes, or fun movie soundtracks that make great backdrops for high-energy games.

I once used Harry Belafonte's "Jump in the Line" from the *Beetlejuice* soundtrack as game show music. Good ol' Harry Belafonte. Who'da thought?

○ **Get your game on.** Nothing adds a little spice to the learning like a competitive edge. While some games pit individuals against each other, it's easy to break the room into teams and make the individuals on stage representatives for those teams. Suddenly, the crowd becomes a cheering section and the stakes are raised for the whole room. I'll occasionally even give individual competitors the chance to win a "consultation" with the rest of their team. Everybody has a laser-focus when the whole crowd knows their teammate could be coming to them for help at any minute. In spite of all this cutthroat competition, keep it on the up and up. No boos for the other team allowed. Only cheering is permitted. And never pit the boys against the girls. That's a recipe for a little more competitive spirit than you bargained for. Not to mention that the girls almost always smoke the boys. It's one of those harsh realities us guys have to deal with.

TAPE WORM! yuck.

TOOT

Method 8:

Team Teaching

Some lessons are talkier than others. That's just the way it is. And while we must constantly infuse lessons with creativity using *The Rule of Three* (see page 72), and push ourselves to hit every learning style, it is a necessary evil that in order to communicate, we sometimes have to run at the mouth. You can add some much-needed variety to lessons that are a bit heavier on lip service by simply breaking up the jibber-jabber between two people.

It Works Like This

Take those pages of chitchat and break them into a dialogue. Take the time to split up the teaching script on paper, so each person knows exactly what he or she is responsible for and what the transitions are.

When you break up dialogue, your natural instinct may be to break the lesson into big chunks. Resist the urge. Instead, keep the back-and-forth flowing. It should feel like the two of you are just hanging out talking. This informal conversational approach to team teaching is very compelling to watch and screams authenticity to kids.

It Looks Like This

Here's a snippet from a lesson that was long on talk. By adapting it for two it became a much more compelling chat.

Before

Aaron: We face a battle everyday as we go through life.

Every time we find ourselves wandering a little further from how God wants us to do life, we are locked in battle with an enemy.

Every time we find ourselves tempted to use foul language, to think the worst about someone else, to selfishly put our own desires above those of other people, we are engaged in hand-to-hand combat with an enemy.

See, it's easy to think these things just happen, that they are just a coincidental part of doing life, but the truth is that there is a very real enemy working against us, trying to lead us, little by little, farther from God and the life God has planned for us.

Our enemy's name is Satan.

Now, it's true that we cannot often see his attacks, but does that mean we are helpless? No. For one, if we have chosen to be in a relationship with God, then God is on our side. And he has equipped us for battle. He has given us armor and weapons to fight with. It is not the kind of armor you can see and touch, like what I'm wearing. But it is very real nonetheless.

The apostle Paul calls it the armor of God.

He says: "Put on the full armor of God, that you may be able to stand firm against the schemes of the devil" (Ephesians 6:11).

Now, the armor of God is made up of several different pieces.

For those of us who are followers of God, for those of us who have chosen to fight on God's side in this battle, we must learn how to use this armor. Every time the enemy attacks you …

When he encourages you to disobey your parents. When he tells you to ignore the new kid who needs a friend. When he makes you think that following your favorite basketball player is more important than following God. Every time the enemy attacks you … you face a choice.

239

AFTER

DUGAN: WE FACE A BATTLE EVERYDAY AS WE GO THROUGH LIFE.

AARON: THAT'S RIGHT. EVERY TIME WE FIND OURSELVES WANDERING A LITTLE FARTHER FROM HOW GOD WANTS US TO DO LIFE, WE ARE LOCKED IN BATTLE WITH AN ENEMY.

DUGAN: EVERY TIME WE FIND OURSELVES TEMPTED TO USE FOUL LANGUAGE, TO THINK THE WORST ABOUT SOMEONE ELSE, TO SELFISHLY PUT OUR OWN DESIRES ABOVE THOSE OF OTHER PEOPLE, WE ARE ENGAGED IN HAND-TO-HAND COMBAT WITH AN ENEMY.

AARON: SEE, IT'S EASY TO THINK THESE THINGS JUST HAPPEN, THAT THEY ARE JUST A COINCIDENTAL PART OF DOING LIFE, BUT THE TRUTH IS THAT THERE IS A VERY REAL ENEMY WORKING AGAINST US, TRYING TO LEAD US, LITTLE BY LITTLE, FARTHER FROM GOD AND THE LIFE GOD HAS PLANNED FOR US.

DUGAN: YEP. OUR ENEMY'S NAME IS SATAN.

AARON: IT'S TRUE THAT WE CANNOT OFTEN SEE HIS ATTACKS, BUT DOES THAT MEAN WE ARE HELPLESS? NO. FOR ONE, IF WE HAVE CHOSEN TO BE IN A RELATIONSHIP WITH GOD, THEN GOD IS ON OUR SIDE. AND HE HAS EQUIPPED US FOR BATTLE.

DUGAN: YEP.

AARON: HE HAS GIVEN US ARMOR AND WEAPONS TO FIGHT WITH. IT IS NOT THE KIND YOU CAN SEE AND TOUCH, LIKE WHAT I'M WEARING. BUT IT IS VERY REAL NONETHELESS.

DUGAN: THE APOSTLE PAUL CALLS IT THE ARMOR OF GOD. HE SAYS: "PUT ON THE FULL ARMOR OF GOD, THAT YOU MAY BE ABLE TO STAND FIRM AGAINST THE SCHEMES OF THE DEVIL" (EPHESIANS 6:11).

AARON: NOW, THE ARMOR OF GOD IS MADE UP OF SEVERAL DIFFERENT PIECES.

DUGAN: A HELMET.

AARON: A SHIELD.

★ ★ ★ ★
"Brilliant! Two thumbs up!"
—Danny Johnson
Sunday School Review Editor,
Chicago Herald

DUGAN: A SWORD.

AARON: A BELT.

DUGAN: A BREASTPLATE.

AARON: A PAIR OF SHOES.

DUGAN: FOR THOSE OF US WHO ARE FOLLOWERS OF GOD, FOR THOSE OF US WHO HAVE CHOSEN TO FIGHT ON GOD'S SIDE IN THIS BATTLE, WE MUST LEARN HOW TO USE THIS ARMOR. EVERY TIME THE ENEMY ATTACKS YOU ...

AARON: WHEN HE ENCOURAGES YOU TO DISOBEY YOUR PARENTS ...

DUGAN: WHEN HE TELLS YOU TO IGNORE THE NEW KID WHO NEEDS A FRIEND ...

AARON: WHEN HE MAKES YOU THINK THAT FOLLOWING YOUR FAVORITE BASKETBALL PLAYER IS MORE IMPORTANT THAN FOLLOWING GOD ...

DUGAN: EVERY TIME THE ENEMY ATTACKS YOU ... YOU FACE A CHOICE.

Helpful Little Hints

○ *Exception, not the rule.* Make team teaching the exception, not the rule. I regularly run into teaching buddies who serve together exclusively. It's great to have such a collaborative spirit, but if this describes you, I encourage you to cut the umbilical cord from one another and go at it alone once in a while.

By *only* team teaching, you're probably leaning into one another, using one another as a crutch. This keeps you from trying out new tools, and from building up the ability to control the room solo. In addition to your own development, you could be robbing the ministry of some much-needed power. If two strong teachers are always paired together, imagine the power the ministry would gain if the two of you broke up. In one fell swoop, you double the impact of your teaching twosome.

So consider splitting up ... at least once in a while. See other people. Other lessons. You can still be friends.

○ *The apprentice.* While we're on the topic of multiplying your collective effectiveness ... you know that teenager you've pegged as having the creative teaching goods? A team teaching lesson is a perfect opportunity to train a new apprentice or give a fledgling teacher a chance to wade in knee-deep, while having the safety-line of a more experienced teacher to help float the burden.

○ *Rehearsal ... it's not just for breakfast anymore.* The key to great team teaching is a seemingly natural chemistry between two people. Believe it or not, this doesn't always happen best ... naturally. It takes rehearsal. While I'm an advocate of rehearsal all the time, it's the mayo that holds the team teaching sandwich together.

Deli analogies aside, use rehearsal to work on picking up each other's cues and knowing when one person is done and it's your turn to talk. Nothing screams unnatural like a Mack-truck-sized gap in the dialogue because you didn't realize the other person was done. Also use rehearsal time to create a natural chemistry between the two of you—the feeling that you are truly having a conversation, a laid-back comfortable energy, rather than a tag-team lecture. Being "teacher-y" in tandem comes off forced and insincere.

Method 9:

Sound Effects

Sound effects (SFX) are an eazy-peezy way to enhance any lesson. The trick is finding good ones and executing them well. So read on. There are lots of hints here for SFX success.

It Works Like This

SFX can enhance something visual—like a roar as Daniel is thrown into an off-stage lion's den. They can create excitement during simple storytelling—like a loud layer of crowd noises in the background as you tell the story of Jesus entering Jerusalem on Palm Sunday. They can be funny—like Scooby Doo–style boinks and bings to go with pratfalls or visual gags. And they can be poignant and gripping—like thunder and wind that stop suddenly when Jesus calms the storm. Bottom line … SFX are a cheap, all-purpose way to add richness and layers to great lessons. So don't be afraid to sound off.

It Looks Like This

Example: Sound Jars
The stage is set with seven jars and bottles of various shapes and sizes. As a setup to the story of Jesus healing the ten lepers and only

one returning to say thanks, the kids are told that "thank you" is sometimes a very hard phrase to say. Practice is required! Explain that you have trapped several "sounds" inside these jars, so they can practice saying this challenging phrase. One by one, the jars are opened, the sounds are "released" ... laughter, crunching of snow, a horse neighing, a baby giggling. In response to each unstoppered sound, the delighted kids are led in a rousing cry of "Thank you, Jesus!"

The sounds, of course, are all on a CD run by a sound guy. He has a clear, visual cue: as the teacher pops each cork, top, or lid, the sound needs to tumble out. The kids—usually kindergarten and first graders—are delighted by these sounds as they pour out of the jars.

Example: Jesus Is Crucified

SFX aren't just for humor and silliness. For the fourth- and fifth-grade set, I often storytell the events around the crucifixion with almost nothing on stage but myself. I don't want to be too graphic (which is why I limit the props I use), but I want them to come face-to-face with the horrible things that happened to my Savior.

When the time comes for Jesus to be nailed to the cross, I mime out this action from the guards' point of view, laying an imaginary Jesus onto the ground on an imaginary cross. But when I kneel to drive the stakes into his hands and feet, I lean into sounds.

As I mime the nailing ... ***TINK* *TINK* *TINK* *TINK*** ... we hear the sound of hammer hitting spike.

Again for the other hand ... ***TINK* *TINK* *TINK* *TINK***

Again for the feet ... ***TINK* *TINK* *TINK* *TINK***

The moment is gripping. Staggering. Holy.

There's nothing on stage but me telling this story. But the kids are riveted and this event comes to life in an amazing way.

A note on delivery: Make sure that you practice with the CD so that your hammering motions actually line up. When the ***TINK*** rings through the room a second or two after you strike your spike ... well, let's just say the moment gets drowned out by bad timing.

Helpful Little Hints

QUACK

○ **Pop culture splash.** Anytime you can incorporate highly recognizable sound bites from pop culture, it's a guaranteed hit. I once told the story of the Lost Sheep by sprinkling in lots of these little bites throughout … a Homer Simpson "d'oh!" here, a snippet of "Who Let the Sheep Out? Baa, ba, ba, ba, ba" (poking fun at the Baha Men hit "Who Let the Dogs Out?") … stuff like that.

SPLAT!

Just be certain that you purchase what you use. While I know it's easy to do, I'm not an advocate of looking the other way when it comes to copyright laws (Jesus probably isn't either, now that you mention it). So buy that stuff before you use it. Even recording it from the original CD is technically a no-no. An easy way around the copyright thing is just to record your own version of it. The phrase "d'oh!" isn't copyrighted, but any sound bite pulled directly from the TV show is. So I record myself doing "d'oh!" in my best Homer rendition. Problem solved.

wizzle wizzle wizzle

BONGGGGGGGGG…

○ **Sound effects sources.** Downloadables are your best bet. Steer clear of any sites that say "Free Sound Effect Downloads." While the price is right, you get what you pay for, and the quality is usually terrible. I've spent too many hours scouring through free sites and finding nothing useable. In the end, it was worth going to a high quality SFX site (plenty are listed in the back of the book) and plopping my $1.40 on the counter for a kickin' T-Rex roar to use for Daniel and the lion's den, or the perfect sound of hammer hitting a metal spike to bring the crucifixion to life. In many ways, that buck and change is an investment because once I buy it, the sound bite is mine, and I get plenty of mileage all over the ministry out of high quality SFX.

WHACK!

BOING

○ **Samplers, DJ mixers, and other things that go boom.** For all of us without scads of tech volunteers, there are other options that can make SFX a one-person operation. Of course, you can have a CD player or boom box on stage with you for easy access, but

KER-FLUNF

CLANG CLANG CLANG

Method 245

this can be cumbersome. Bending down to hunt for the "play" button takes the magic out of the moment, plus there's usually a several-second lag between the moment you hit play and the moment the SFX sounds off.

Another option is a sampler or a DJ mixer machine. While these gizmos take a little bit of know-how, once you figure them out, they make smooth SFX a breeze. They give you the ability to directly upload or transfer sound files

(kind of like a really big iPod), programmable easy-press buttons, and the ability to wire it into an existing sound system. This makes a sampler or DJ mixer the perfect gift for the teacher who has ... no tech person. (Check out page 319 in the Appendix ... that's the stuff at the back of the book ... for details on where to find these cool high-tech doodads.)

○ *Timing is everything.* Here's a hint for smooth execution. Cue up to the right track, hit play, let the CD spin, and a millisecond before the sound effect rolls, hit pause. That way, when you hit play, the sound is immediate. Have your sound specialist (or your spouse) do this for all the SFX in the lesson, cueing up each one while you're talking. For more cue smoothness, print your SFX assistant a cue sheet ... here's what mine usually looks like:

246 8, WHO DO WE APPRECIATE? PENGUINS! PENGUINS! YAY!

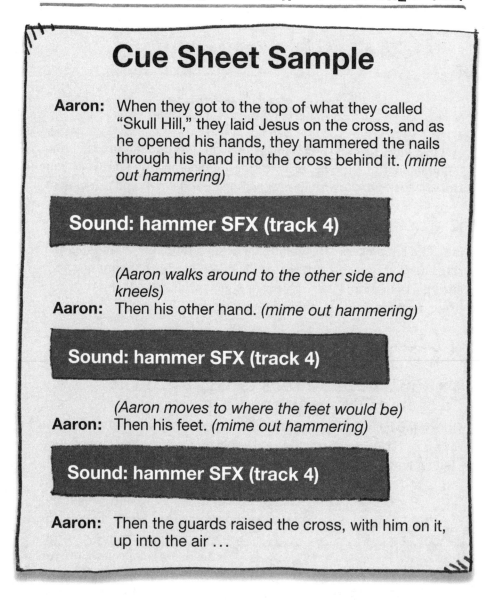

Cue Sheet Sample

Aaron: When they got to the top of what they called "Skull Hill," they laid Jesus on the cross, and as he opened his hands, they hammered the nails through his hand into the cross behind it. *(mime out hammering)*

Sound: hammer SFX (track 4)

(Aaron walks around to the other side and kneels)
Aaron: Then his other hand. *(mime out hammering)*

Sound: hammer SFX (track 4)

(Aaron moves to where the feet would be)
Aaron: Then his feet. *(mime out hammering)*

Sound: hammer SFX (track 4)

Aaron: Then the guards raised the cross, with him on it, up into the air ...

That way, there's no chance for confusion on the timing or forgetting which track number the hammer was on. Because, when it comes to sensational SFX, timing is everything.

BOOOOO-
WAAAAAA
FOG
HORN

Method 10:

Soundtracks

Movie soundtracks are created specifically to underscore the emotional impact of a movie. A little mood music may be just what your story needs to orchestrate a captivating ... and emotional ... moment.

It Works Like This

Even the simplest of storytelling takes on a rich new layer when stirring music underscores the scene. Just tell the story or combine audience participation, visual props, or some other creative method, but bring music under the scene as the story begins.

It Looks Like This

Example: *The Prince of Egypt* in the Garden of Gethsemane

One of my favorite all-purpose music scores is track eight from *The Prince of Egypt* soundtrack. I've used it many times in simple storytelling lessons, including the story of Jesus in the garden of Gethsemane. With no props, no audience participation, nothing but me storytelling and reenacting the story, this music brings the whole scene to life ... from Jesus' struggle and prayer, to the entrance of the angry mob, to Peter chopping off the official's ear, to Jesus' acceptance of the arrest

... this track has got all the highs and lows you need for this story ... and gobs more.

Example: Soundtracks ... they're not just for stories anymore

Once, when faced with creatively explaining the Bridge Illustration for a salvation lesson, I decided to use a range of funky art supplies. I drew out the Bridge Illustration on a four-foot-by-eight-foot sheet of plywood. Using scrapers, paint, and other unexpected supplies, I sketched out our relationship with God in an artsy and unexpected way. And while compelling, it felt slightly flat. Something was missing.

Music! I tried it again, this time adding an odd, whirring percussive soundtrack to the message (track one from the 1999 Blue Man Group CD *Audio*). It was a whole new experience. The driving force of the music propelled and energized the telling of this important concept, and the kids were mesmerized by the salvation message so clearly illustrated in an unexpected way.

Helpful Little Hints

○ **Soundtrack sources.** Where am I getting all this music, you ask? To get you off and running, check out the original movie soundtracks to *Batman*, *Henry V*, *The Prince of Egypt*, *The Lord of the Rings*, and all three Blue Man Group CDs. These soundtracks are custom-designed for the purpose of great storytelling. And as long as you're playing it off the original CD and not charging admission (you're not, are you?), then you're on pretty safe turf as far as copyrights go.

There's also stuff called "production music" (the kind of generic music beds that often get used for commercials, documentaries, and videos). Don't turn your nose up at these no-name tunes ... they can be a rich resource. Production music is often composed with the sole purpose of capturing a specific mood or flavor or region. Jump to the Appendix (pages 318–319) for websites that will score you some great downloadable production music.

○ *Finding the flow.* When trying to find a track for a specific story, start by listening to the first little bit of several tracks from promising CDs, like the ones listed above. If it doesn't capture the mood you want in the first few seconds, move on. Once you ID a track with the right vibe, try reading your story along with it. Remember, in most cases you only need three to five minutes of music, so it doesn't matter if the whole 15-minute track doesn't groove exactly right. As you read, don't rush. Follow the emotional ups and downs of the music—look for places you can be silent and let the music do the work for you, listen in for possible spots to add action. You'll be amazed at how often movie music feels like it was written with your story in mind.

○ *Method 11:* ○ ○

The Voice from Beyond

Remember sitting in school and suddenly the PA system would blare a staticky voice requesting Mrs. Whats-Her-Name send So-and-So to the principal's office? There's something cool and unexpected about that disembodied voice breaking into the lesson. Well, now you can add another character or teacher into the mix from the outside world, without adding another person ... using a prerecorded voice.

It Works Like This

Figure out who you'd like to talk to during your lesson. Maybe it's a second teacher in a remote location. Maybe it's a "celebrity." Maybe it's a Bible character you want to have a real-time chat with.

Then figure out how you'll reach them. By walkie-talkie? By phone? Two cans tied together with a string?

Now record the voice of the character, and you're all set to play the voice and have a seemingly spontaneous heart-to-heart with your unseen pal.

It Looks Like This

WALKIE
TALKIE
DUCKY

Example: Walkie-Talkie Teacher

An easy way to introduce a disembodied extra teacher is via walkie-talkie. In a camp themed unit called "Camp Iwilligoway," my writing partner and I wanted to bring in another character, a ranger who could report on happenings "elsewhere" in the camp and help us introduce the topic and story each week. But we were short on volunteers who could commit to a multiple-week unit. So we created Ranger Dax, a character the kids would never see but whom the teacher would talk to every week via walkie-talkie. After writing the lessons, we brought in a volunteer for a one-shot recording session of every Ranger Dax segment. Laying a staticky walkie-talkie effect over the voice didn't require much work. And *presto!* We had our prerecorded man-in-the-woods, ready to yak with the teacher every week. At the end of each Dax segment, we held up the walkie-talkie for the kids to say goodbye to Dax, always to thunderous response. There was no doubt ... the kids thought Dax was real and they couldn't wait to hear from him.

Example: Phone-a-Friend

In the game show *Who Wants to Be a Millionaire?* contestants are given a phone-a-friend option to help them figure out questions. How about letting kids contact a celebrity for help during a game show? By calling up these characters and putting them on "speaker phone," you've got a whole world of voice-over possibilities at your disposal. Over the years I've called the Crocodile Hunter, the Taco Bell dog, Michael Jordan, and Homer Simpson, all from the middle of my teaching stage. The phone wasn't even plugged in.

MOSES HERE,
WITH THE
TOP TEN ...

Or how about calling a Bible character for a gab session? This is a great way to adapt a Bible drama or storytelling script that may involve scads of actors when you're the only creative volunteer on hand. Simply call Moses from the stage, having him give you a play by play, in modern language, about his little face-off with Pharaoh.

This works best with kids second grade and older, so there's no confusion about whether or not this is the *real* Moses on the phone. While younger kids may wonder, these older kids understand this isn't real, but it's a fun way to get information about a story, seemingly firsthand.

Helpful Little Hints

○ ***Recording things right.*** There are a couple ways you can record these types of voice-overs: you can put them all in one chunk, with timed spaces for the teacher to talk, or you can break up each section onto a separate track. With practice, you can get the timing of the one-track option, but I'm a fan of putting each phrase from the character on a separate track. When doing it this way, break the tracks by every time the live teacher speaks, except for the smallest responses.

So, for example, a conversation with Ranger Dax might be laid out like this:

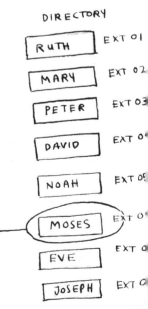

DIRECTORY

RUTH	EXT 01
MARY	EXT 02
PETER	EXT 03
DAVID	EXT 0
NOAH	EXT 0
MOSES	EXT 0
EVE	EXT 0
JOSEPH	EXT 0

[Play Track 1]

Dax: Home base, home base?

Live Teacher: Whoa, hold that thought campers. Hey, that's gotta be Ranger Dax! (Talk to kids while getting walkie-talkie.) If you didn't meet him last week he's in charge of animal rescue and tracking in the forest around Camp Iwilligoway. I bet he knows you guys are here and wants to tell you about our secret animal for this week.
Roger, Dax this is home base. How are you buddy?

[Play Track 2]

Dax: Oh, I'm okay. Got myself in a bit of a pickle first thing this morning and I'm just trying to get back on track.

Live Teacher: *(Into walkie-talkie)* Roger that, Dax. What's goin' on?

[Play Track 3]

Dax: Well, I'm a little embarrassed to admit it, but I got lost. I took a wrong turn off the trail this morning and ended up smack-dab in the middle of Briar's Gulch.
Weirdest thing ... a bunch of the trail marker posts seem to have gone missing.

Live Teacher: Uh, I'm sorry Dax, I used 'em last week to show our campers something. I'm really sorry about that. Do you need me to send out the dogs to find you?

[Play Track 4]

Dax: So that's it, is it? Well, no harm done. Between me and Bubba, we sniffed our way out again. I'm back on track now.

Live Teacher: That's good. Well, we were wondering if you have our animal for this week?

… and so on.

Again, if you don't have somebody to press play on the CD player all those times, it may be easier to record everything to one track and leave space between your character's lines for the live teacher to talk. But this separate-track treatment gives you the most control over the conversation.

Method 12:
Showing Signs

For older kids who can read, sometimes no talking is required. This quirky convention lets you puts all the words into writing, while the kids read along.

It Works Like This

Why talk when you can hold up signs to say what's on your mind? I know, it sounds weird, but this unexpected style of storytelling is really quite compelling.

There are a couple different ways to put this method into practice. The first involves one or more teachers holding handwritten signs to deliver their dialogue and flipping from card to card. The second approach requires using toys to create photographed scenes you'll add text to, comic-book-style. Scratching your head yet? Well, let's illustrate this hard-to-imagine method by example.

It Looks Like This

Example: Placards

After seeing a production of *Blue Man Group* (a funky live stage show that originated in Chicago), my team and I were struck by how much creative communication was possible without ever speaking. The Blue Men never talk. The entire show is done without a spoken word, but in one sequence, the blue boys need to talk to each other. So they carry on a conversation by holding up a series of prewritten placards. They dialogue in this manner for about five or six minutes, flipping forward their cards one by one to reveal each new phrase or sentence. What a great idea!

This inspiration led to a nonverbal storytelling sequence for our children's ministry, using prewritten cards. Two teachers stand side by side and "talk" in this card-flipping way. They each hold a stack of cards and, in response to one another, drop the front card to reveal

the next. Timing is a critical component with this quirky convention, as you have to allow time for the audience to read each card. Our first foray into this creative tool was a sketch for adults attending a children's ministry conference. It showcases the dialogue between a children's ministry leader and the various members of her team.

Here's a snapshot. Remember, these lines are written on large cards, not spoken. Each new line represents a new card.

It has a "silent movie" kind of feel. You could easily apply this method to Bible storytelling as well. How about the dialogue between Jesus and Satan in the wilderness? Or Cain and Abel? Any story that involves two or more people talking to each other can be put to paper in this way. There's something unexpected about putting your words on cards rather than speaking, and the kids really respond.

Example: Toy Stories

I once saw a guy who created the entire Noah's Ark story out of LEGOs. Using LEGO people and parts from multiple sets, he built a series of little LEGO scenes and took digital photos of his handiwork. By adding the appropriate Bible passage and occasional speech bubbles for the characters (you could use PowerPoint or Photoshop to insert this text), he created an ingenious slideshow presentation any fourth-grader would be enraptured by.

While this LEGO masterpiece was elaborate and involved, the idea itself is simple. Using action figures, Playmobil sets, Weebles, Mighty Beanz, even PEZ dispensers, you can create funky little Bible vignettes, photograph them, upload them into Photoshop or PowerPoint, and add Bible verse subtitles and speech bubbles.

The result? An inventive slideshow-style performance, and a quirky and compelling way to tell any Bible story ... no talking required.

Helpful Little Hints

○ *Music to your ears.* While this silent treatment of storytelling is very cool, there's something unsettling about sitting in total silence while your teachers flip their cards or while you watch this off-beat slideshow. Underscore either of these approaches with a little music to put everyone at ease. Pick music that maximizes the kooky mood. This method is a little wacky, so even popular songs with lyrics (try the *Shrek* soundtrack, for example), can lend the right tone to this off-the-wall way of teaching.

USE ME! USE ME! ME! ME! ME! ME! ME!

PLEA

○ *Readers only, please.* Remember, this method requires reading, so limit its use to the older kids in the ministry. Adults also respond well to it, so it's easily adapted for ministry-wide events or volunteer celebrations.

boing boing boing

Method 13:

Motions and Phrases

This tool is ideal for combining with visual props for a three-way whammy that hits auditory, visual, and kinesthetic learners right where it counts.

It Works Like This

Break the story into sections and attach a different phrase and motion to each part. These phrases and motions get the learning in our bodies, which is great for retention. If the phrases rhyme or have some other hook that helps them stay memorable, all the better.

And don't forget to repeatedly run back to the top of the routine and challenge the kids to speed through the whole cycle. It becomes a memory challenge with kids and puts a competitive edge on the whole experience, which is especially fun for those older boys who need a place to focus all that ... shall we say ... energy.

It Looks Like This

Example: David and Goliath

In this version of the classic showdown between hulk and half-pint, the phrases and motions give each part of the story a memorable handle. I usually add a prop at each story segment. I'll go to the prop, unveil it for the kids, and tell what happened in this part of the story. Then, I'll teach the phrase and motion for this segment. After getting a few under our belts, we'll run back to the top and try to put them all together.

Here's the rundown on the phrases and motions for this story:

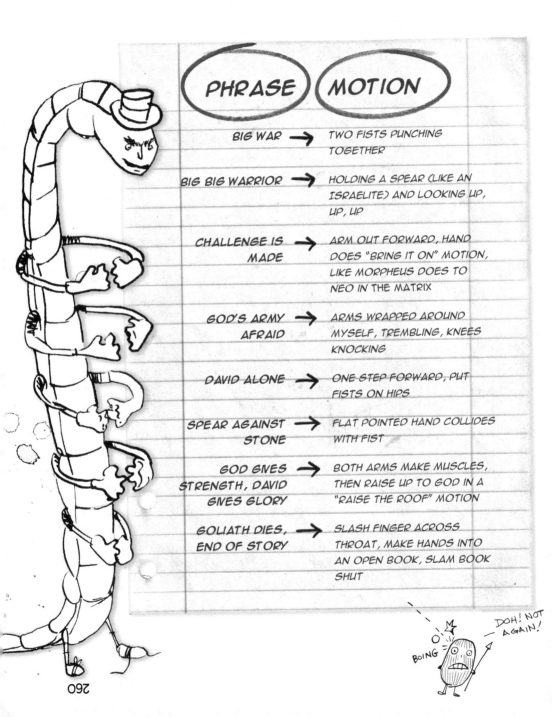

PHRASE	MOTION
BIG WAR →	TWO FISTS PUNCHING TOGETHER
BIG BIG WARRIOR →	HOLDING A SPEAR (LIKE AN ISRAELITE) AND LOOKING UP, UP, UP
CHALLENGE IS MADE →	ARM OUT FORWARD, HAND DOES "BRING IT ON" MOTION, LIKE MORPHEUS DOES TO NEO IN THE MATRIX
GOD'S ARMY AFRAID →	ARMS WRAPPED AROUND MYSELF, TREMBLING, KNEES KNOCKING
DAVID ALONE →	ONE STEP FORWARD, PUT FISTS ON HIPS
SPEAR AGAINST STONE →	FLAT POINTED HAND COLLIDES WITH FIST
GOD GIVES STRENGTH, DAVID GIVES GLORY →	BOTH ARMS MAKE MUSCLES, THEN RAISE UP TO GOD IN A "RAISE THE ROOF" MOTION
GOLIATH DIES, END OF STORY →	SLASH FINGER ACROSS THROAT, MAKE HANDS INTO AN OPEN BOOK, SLAM BOOK SHUT

BOING   O!   DOH! NOT AGAIN!

Example: Run Through the Bible

I first heard my buddy Bob Gustafson teach the whole Bible like this over 11 years ago, and I still remember his phrases by heart. He breaks the whole Bible into a whirlwind of excitement with this custom-made set of phrases and motions:

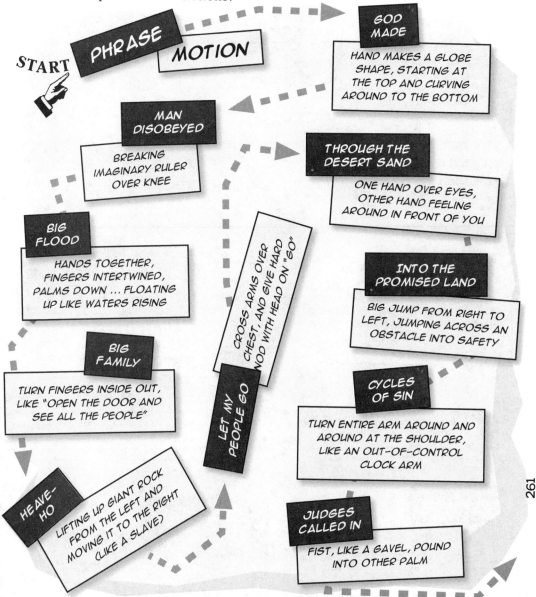

START

PHRASE

MOTION

GOD MADE
HAND MAKES A GLOBE SHAPE, STARTING AT THE TOP AND CURVING AROUND TO THE BOTTOM

MAN DISOBEYED
BREAKING IMAGINARY RULER OVER KNEE

THROUGH THE DESERT SAND
ONE HAND OVER EYES, OTHER HAND FEELING AROUND IN FRONT OF YOU

BIG FLOOD
HANDS TOGETHER, FINGERS INTERTWINED, PALMS DOWN ... FLOATING UP LIKE WATERS RISING

INTO THE PROMISED LAND
BIG JUMP FROM RIGHT TO LEFT, JUMPING ACROSS AN OBSTACLE INTO SAFETY

BIG FAMILY
TURN FINGERS INSIDE OUT, LIKE "OPEN THE DOOR AND SEE ALL THE PEOPLE"

LET MY PEOPLE GO
CROSS ARMS OVER CHEST, AND GIVE HARD NOD WITH HEAD ON "GO"

CYCLES OF SIN
TURN ENTIRE ARM AROUND AND AROUND AT THE SHOULDER, LIKE AN OUT-OF-CONTROL CLOCK ARM

HEAVE-HO
LIFTING UP GIANT ROCK FROM THE LEFT AND MOVING IT TO THE RIGHT (LIKE A SLAVE)

JUDGES CALLED IN
FIST, LIKE A GAVEL, POUND INTO OTHER PALM

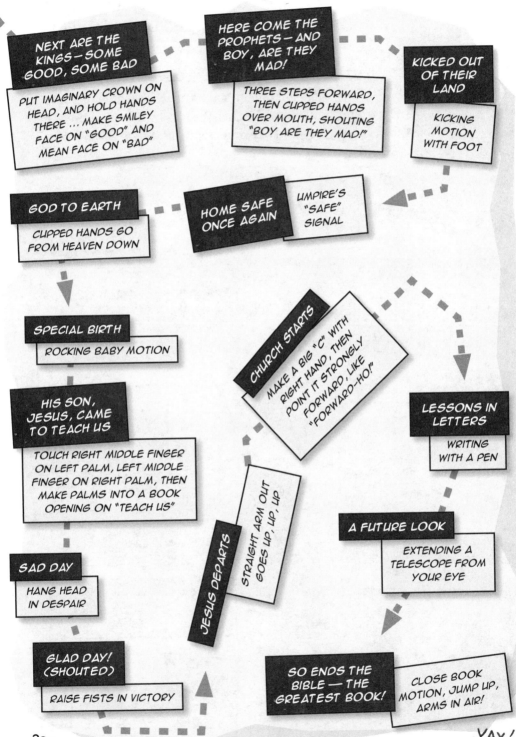

NEXT ARE THE KINGS—SOME GOOD, SOME BAD

PUT IMAGINARY CROWN ON HEAD, AND HOLD HANDS THERE ... MAKE SMILEY FACE ON "GOOD" AND MEAN FACE ON "BAD"

HERE COME THE PROPHETS—AND BOY, ARE THEY MAD!

THREE STEPS FORWARD, THEN CUPPED HANDS OVER MOUTH, SHOUTING "BOY ARE THEY MAD!"

KICKED OUT OF THEIR LAND

KICKING MOTION WITH FOOT

GOD TO EARTH

CUPPED HANDS GO FROM HEAVEN DOWN

HOME SAFE ONCE AGAIN

UMPIRE'S "SAFE" SIGNAL

SPECIAL BIRTH

ROCKING BABY MOTION

CHURCH STARTS

MAKE A BIG "C" WITH RIGHT HAND, THEN POINT IT STRONGLY FORWARD, LIKE "FORWARD-HO!"

LESSONS IN LETTERS

WRITING WITH A PEN

HIS SON, JESUS, CAME TO TEACH US

TOUCH RIGHT MIDDLE FINGER ON LEFT PALM, LEFT MIDDLE FINGER ON RIGHT PALM, THEN MAKE PALMS INTO A BOOK OPENING ON "TEACH US"

JESUS DEPARTS

STRAIGHT ARM OUT GOES UP, UP, UP

A FUTURE LOOK

EXTENDING A TELESCOPE FROM YOUR EYE

SAD DAY

HANG HEAD IN DESPAIR

GLAD DAY! (SHOUTED)

RAISE FISTS IN VICTORY

SO ENDS THE BIBLE — THE GREATEST BOOK!

CLOSE BOOK MOTION, JUMP UP, ARMS IN AIR!

YAY!

Helpful Little Hints

○ ***Go with the flow.*** When creating your own motions for stories, make sure the ending position of one motion flows easily into the next. Remember, after you get a few phrases into the story, you'll want to run back to the top and try to speed through it. If the motions don't flow well one into the other, the whole thing starts to get disjointed and spiral out of control.

○ ***Strong like bull.*** Boys often don't like to participate in this kind of moving and grooving teaching. And with good reason. Girly motions. No boy in his right mind wants to wave his arms over his head like a little daffodil blowing in the breeze. So make those motions strong and manly! Don't worry about the girls ... they'll go along with it, no problem.

Need help coming up with manly motions? Draft a teenage boy to help you think them up. Make sure he forces you to create motions he'd be comfortable doing. In fact, take it a step further and have that same teenager help you teach them during the lessons. Nothing will put your fourth-grade boys in motion like seeing the 16-year-old guy with the three earrings getting his Bible groove on.

> SIR, STRONG LIKE BULL, SIR, NO GIRLIE MOTIONS, SIR

Method 14:

Simply Messy

Being raised on Nickelodeon and early episodes of *DoubleDare* has taught me one thing: kids love a mess. But in Sunday school, our fear of the janitor often causes us to keep our creative thinking neatly in the "mess-free" zone.

It Works Like This

Plastic tarps are cheap, so there's no reason not to make a mess. The most important thing is to not let the mess take on a life of it's own ... don't do mess exclusively for fun or for filler, but make sure you drive all that messy creativity around clarifying the biblical concept you're teaching. All the slime, gak, shaving cream, and chocolate pudding in the world won't do you any good if, at the end of the day, the Bible concept is a jumbled mess in kids' minds.

It Looks Like This

Example: Slimy Surprises

In a 101-level lesson on creation for second and third graders, I wanted to do a preemptive strike on evolution. While many of them hadn't been taught the Darwin dogma in school yet, the day was fast approaching, and I wanted to prepare them.

We created a little game called "Slime or Not!" My contestants were three "scientists" (really some scripted volunteers in white lab coats), and they were asked a series of questions about the creation of humans. Professor Slimenheimer professed that when a slimy pool was heated up millions of years ago, it created life. Bottom line? People came from slime.

The judges gave him the bong, the host pulled a handle, and a bucket of slime dumped over his head.

It was Professor 2's turn: Professor E.Z. Monkeyshine claimed humans simply evolved from monkeys, all by accident. Again, the judges hit the buzzer, and Dr. Monkeyshine got the slime treatment.

Finally, Professor 3 was up: Dr. M. T. Theory, panicked by the consequences doled out upon his colleagues, picked up a nearby Bible and read from Genesis. Correct response! He was saved from the sliming of a lifetime.

A great setup for a lesson on creation, and good prep for refuting various scientific theories, the slime station was easy to concoct. I built a very simple booth, kind of like a carnival booth. From the horizontal crossbeam overhead (a big sign that read "Slime or Not!" covered it from the front), I rigged two tipable buckets (remember, Professor 3 never gets slimed). I ran a cord from each bucket, so when I pulled the cord, the bucket tipped onto the white-clad scientist sitting below.

Don't forget to tarp down the teaching area. The between-service cleanup required for this little slime-fest was well worth the kids astounded faces and the attention it bought me for the rest of my creation content.

SLIMEROO

MY COUSIN IS AN APE, I TELL YOU!

SLIME COMING RIGHT UP

Example: Shaving Cream Wall

I once told the Bridge Illustration for a salvation lesson in kind of a funky way. I suspended a three-foot-by-five-foot sheet of Plexiglas from the ceiling tiles and drew out the Bridge Illustration in advance with black-light paint (you can find the stuff at some hardware stores). I then covered the entire image with shaving cream (three cans do the job nicely). When the salvation message began, we dimmed the lights, hit the Plexiglas with a black light, and rolled cool music as I told the salvation story. I used a squeegee to squeege away the shaving cream, one section at a time. As each section of shaving cream was cleared away, the black light hit the black-light paint, making the salvation story pop with glow-in-the-dark power. It was funky, effective, and perfect for the fifth-grade crowd I was teaching.

Helpful Little Hints

○ *A recipe for mess.* Store-bought slime can be expensive, so rustling up enough of the glutinous goo to dump over someone's head could break the bank. Here's my money-saving recipe for the sludgy stuff ... it's actually a crêpes batter recipe, but it makes great slime that splats wonderfully when it hits:

QUICHE LORRAINE

frozen deep dish pie crus~~t~~
margerine
½ C. ~~cheese~~
½ C. che~~ese~~ ~~pa~~rmesan cheese
1 tbsp. gra~~ted~~
2 tbsp. ~~f~~
4 egg~~s~~
1 t~~sp.~~ salt
1~~½~~. half/half melted butter
Mix cheeses and flour. Mix ~~i~~ ~~fr~~ied bacon/
and milk. Line pie shell with ~~s~~ cheese mixture
raw mushrooms sliced. Then add cheese mixture
then milk mixture. Bake at 375° 30 min and
350° for another 15

NOT QUICHE!! SLIME!

Slime

4 cups water
4 cups milk
16 eggs
8 cups flour

16 TBL margarine, melted
1-oz. bottle green food coloring (not the little bottle from the 4-pack — you can buy larger bottles ~~don't like vanilla extra~~ (like vanilla extract bottles) all of one color.

Mix the water, milk, and eggs in a bucket with an electric mixer. Add in flour, one cup at a time, while mixing. Stir in margarine mix in food coloring.

Makes enough to thoroughly slime one person. Keep refrigerated until slime time.

○ **_Perfect plastic tarping._** Before getting messy, be sure to coat the floor with a simple plastic tarp. You don't have to use that ugly blue crinkly kind either … most home improvement centers (like Home Depot) carry various sizes of clear plastic tarps in the paint section. Just lay it out, cut it to size with scissors, and tape it down with duct tape or gaffers tape.

On the shaving cream wall, I tarped the floor directly beneath me with clear plastic, and I threw the excess shaving cream on the floor as I went, making post-service cleanup a snap. With the slime booth, I knew the splat-factor was going to be high, so I tarped off the entire stage area.

Method 15:

Moving Target

AND...

This is one of the few methods that requires more than one teacher, but it works great with teens or new teachers up front and is a great place to introduce them into the mix.

It Works Like This

Imagine popcorn heating up on your teaching platform. You're never quite sure when the next kernel is going to pop or where it's going to come from. The popping seems random, sporadic, always keeps you guessing.

Now imagine the popcorn kernels are actually teachers. Maybe four or five of them. The stage is darkened, and the teachers are placed all over the stage, even moving from one location to another. When each teacher speaks, a tight pool of light hits them, but when they are done, their light fades, only to have a new light come up on another teacher in another location. They are storytelling together, each taking a line or two and then verbally passing the teaching baton to another. The light directs our eyes where to look, constantly shifting our focus and leaving us guessing where the next bit of the story will come from. This is the "Moving Target." And it makes for irresistible storytelling.

It Looks Like This

...NOW...

Example: HistoryMakers

This HistoryMakers lesson is about the mission of the early church: to change the world by telling everyone about Jesus. They

268

were making history. When we first created this lesson in my children's ministry, we wanted a stage that reflected a gritty real-world kind of look, even a little urban and edgy. We also wanted to create lots of possibility of levels and variety of teaching spaces. So we set up the stage with all kinds of stuff ... a three-level metal painter's scaffold ... a chain-link fence teachers could stand behind ... a freestanding basketball hoop where a teacher could lean or rest against the pole ... garbage cans for sitting on ... lots of stuff to provide interest and levels.

Because the lights are in constant motion, we had to set six predetermined spots teachers would teach from and that we could light with light pools. That's all the lighting we had for making this work, and a moving spotlight wouldn't be effective. So each teacher moved in the darkness from one location to another to wait for their next line.

Additionally, because we wanted the fourth and fifth graders we were teaching to really own this idea of being HistoryMakers themselves, we used teenagers to do all the teaching. This gave the lesson a youthful, relatable, decidedly un-teacher-y air we hoped would bring the content closer to home.

The power of the lesson was palpable.

This one is hard to picture, so here's a sample of it in action. I've included the light cues, so you can see how the movement works. Remember, the lights come up on the teachers and then go off, reappearing on the new teacher at a new location. Each new light cue redirects the kids' attention. Also note the use of music in a strategic spot.

269

Lights: up with location 1

Teacher 1:
For three years, Jesus' entire life had been about his mission.

Lights: down with 1, up with location 2

Teacher 2:
With everyone he met, everywhere he met them.

Lights: down 2, up 1

Teacher 1:
He preached it, taught it, breathed it, performed miracles to prove it, and believed so strongly in it that he gave his life for it.

Lights: down with 1, up with location 3

Teacher 3:
Jesus knew he had to leave the Earth for a while, but he wasn't about to take the mission with him.

Lights: down with 3, up with location 4

Teacher 4:
He wanted to pass it on so that while he was gone, the world was changing and getting ready for his return.

Lights: down with 4, up with location 5

Teacher 5:
So on the day he was going to leave, Jesus gathered his followers on a hill to *(gather around Jesus)* tell them what he had been thinking. *(looking up)* He said:

Sound: fade up music here (Blue Man Group, track 4)

Lights: keep 5 up, bring up location 6

Teacher 1 as Jesus: *(putting on Jesus robe, he's up on scaffolding)* My friends and followers, I'm going to leave you for a while to get things ready in heaven, but don't worry, I'm coming back for you soon. And while I'm gone, you need to take over my mission. I need you to tell my story.
Tell everyone you can about why I came to Earth and what I was about, tell them about my death and resurrection, tell them how they can be in a relationship with God.
I need you to go into all the world and tell my story. Go into Jerusalem and tell them, go into Judea and tell them, go into Samaria, and go to the ends of the earth.

Teacher 4:
He told them how to build the church.

Lights: down with 6 (5 still up)

Lights: fade up with 6
(5 still up)

Teacher 1 as Jesus: Make disciples out of all the nations of the world. Baptize them in my name and teach them to obey everything I've commanded you.

Lights: down with 6

Teacher 3: And he told them about a gift that would authorize and empower them to do it.

Lights: fade up with 6

Teacher 1 as Jesus: Now, don't leave Jerusalem, but wait for the gift of the Holy Spirit that my Father has promised to send you. And I promise to be with you always, to the very end of time.

Sound: music fades out

Lights: fade down with 6

Teacher 2: (*wait till Jesus' light is out*) He told them how to become the very first . . .

ALL: (*look at audience*) History Makers.

Lights: blackout

Not only was direct information delivered to the audience, but notice also how easily an actual scene recreation (like the Jesus scene) can be smoothly woven in. The teacher takes on the part of Jesus just by adding a robe. This popcorn approach can be used powerfully with any narrative-driven story, but also works great with a more concept-driven teaching lesson. Just break up the lesson into multiple parts and start moving that target!

Helpful Little Hint

○ ***Lighting a moving target.*** Don't be thrown by the intimidating tech being wielded in this example. Yes, lighting is absolutely essential to the power of this approach. It just doesn't work if you've got the fluorescent lights up and everyone can see the teachers hustling from one location to another.

But how about this for a do-able adaptation: six different lamps scattered around the stage? The teachers move around to their various locations, and when it's their turn to talk, they click on their lamp. They click it off when they're done and another one clicks on elsewhere, redirecting the focus. You could use lamps from home or even use cheap clip-on workshop lamps like you can buy at Home Depot.

The essence of this tool is the unexpected focus shifts. So no worries … there's a light at the end of the tech tunnel.

Method 16:

Around the Room

For some reason, we automatically default to teaching our kids from the stage or from the front of the room. We almost never question it, do we? But even in the smallest of teaching spaces, there's room for lots of other possibilities!

It Works Like This

What if we bring the lesson into the round? Or we teach from the outside of the room, with the kids surrounded by the story? These simple shifts in how we use space can change a lesson from vanilla to vitalized!

It Looks Like This

Example: In the Round

Story-driven lessons work great in the round. Tape off a "stage" in the center of the room using duct or gaffers tape. Like this:

When the kids come in, have them sit around the circle, surrounding your makeshift stage. Now reenact the story of Jesus healing the paralytic, with them totally immersed in the story.

Example: The Runway

A variation on the in-the-round version ... a runway approach. Tape out the round stage in the middle, but this time, instead of closing the circle, tape out a path ... a runway ... going in opposite directions. Like this:

Now you've got some real space to bring a story to life. Put the Israelites up the far left runway and the Philistines up the far right one, and let David and his nine-foot nemesis take center stage.

HIIIII-YA!

MUNCHKINS.

MUNCHKINS

WHERE'S THE RUNWAY?!

Example: Around the Rim

How about teaching from around the rim of the room? This works great if you're using prop stations to teach a sequence of events. Just line them up around the room, as shown below (X marks the props).

Now, start at one prop and work your way around the outer rim as you teach them through the sequence. Don't worry that the kids will have to scooch around to see you as you move from place to place … it's all part of the plan to keep them engaged and make the learning experiential.

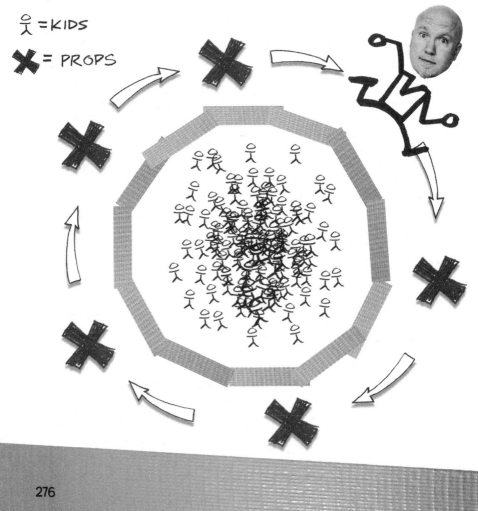

= KIDS

= PROPS

Example: Popcorn

This last one requires more than one teacher. You can do it with two, but it also works great with up to four. Think of it like the Moving Target, only instead of being in front of the kids, you've got the kids surrounded. Set up teachers around the room, like this:

Now, switch off bits of teaching or dialogue between Teacher 1 and the others. The teaching will be popping around them like popcorn, leaving them shifting in their seats and turning to the next voice in the mix. Don't feel the need to go in order. Shake up the order so they never know where the next section is coming from. When using just two teachers, keep the teachers in motion, changing spots while the kids are focused on the teacher that's speaking.

Don't forget to use levels too! Sit on a stool when telling of Jesus instructing the religious leaders in the temple, or climb a ladder when storytelling about Satan taking Jesus up to the mountaintop. This method works great when you add props into the popcorn mix.

Helpful Little Hint

○ *Backing it up.* When using your space creatively like this, you're going to run into times when your back is to some of the kids. Don't worry about it! We have trained ourselves to think that our backs should never face the group, but it's perfectly okay in this setting. It actually draws kids in all the more, as you teach to one side and then intentionally bring the teaching around to the other.

And don't start spinning like a top trying to hit every kid with every sentence. You'll get dizzy going in circles like that! Rather, teach one side for a minute or more, then find another area to focus on, sometimes moving to the opposite side from where you were just facing, rather than following the curve of the circle.

Method 17:
The Live Feed Fake-Out

This method requires a little video know-how, but for teachers who are itching to rev up that new video camera, this might be just the ticket.

It Works Like This

The gimmick that makes this video different from just another on-screen segment is the fun little fake-out involved. It's a lot like a video version of the Ranger Dax voice-over in *The Voice from Beyond* (page 250). The trick is to create a video that allows the live teacher to seemingly dialogue real time with a character on the screen.

It Looks Like This

Example: The Truth Webcast

In *The Truth,* a unit for older kids that covered some hot topics like evolution and the occult, I wanted the ability to bring in oodles of statistics and facts without boring the kids into a catatonic stupor. So we dialed into "Truth Central" via webcast (video), connecting to an "expert" with a plethora of facts and figures right at his fingertips. Our on-camera expert was surrounded by computers and screens and books and could unearth any facts we needed in a heartbeat ... ideal for pulling up research-driven data about the fossil record in our evolution discussion.

The real *Truth* was that there was no live webcast at all. It was all on video, shot with scripted breaks in the on-camera dialogue so the live teacher could insert their teaching points, questions, or address the kids. During those moments of on-camera silence, the "expert" still focused on the camera lens, nodding and giving the incredibly real illusion he was listening along real time. The lesson was a big hit with the kids, who loved that we had the technological talent to bring an expert into Sunday school.

Example: Talking Live to Bible Big Dogs

In a story-driven game show called "Big Dogs," we wanted the kids to be able to hear first-person accounts of Bible stories directly from the Bible Big Dogs themselves. Using the power of video, the teacher conducted newscaster-style interviews with each character via video-link. This offered the option of hearing the story of Ruth directly from Boaz, Naomi, and Ruth herself, giving us unique perspectives on different parts of the story from a first-person point of view. The Bible characters were in a variety of settings (I think Naomi was in a Starbucks drinking a venti mocha latte), as we tuned in to hear their up-close-and-personal accounts.

Again, this wasn't live at all but shot in advance via video. Once more, we used preplanned gaps in the Bible character's dialogue and answers, allowing for scripted responses and commentary by the teacher in the room.

Helpful Little Hints

○ **Ways to keep it easy.** If you've ever worked with video, you know there's no limit to how complicated you can make your project. Editing is a very time-consuming process, one that leaves many people not wanting to open the lid on making videos in the first place. But right-sizing the project can give you an end result that works well, without pulling an all-nighter.

This type of "person on the street" shooting frees you up to shoot things simply. For example, when shooting *The Truth* video, we did it without editing at all. The webcam look gave us permission to keep it on-the-cheap, so we set a camera on a tripod near my computer station, hit "record," and shot it all it one chunk. I had a buddy off-camera mouthing the words the live teacher would say, so the timing would be right, and I just jumped in on cue. It took a few takes to get it right, but it was worth the taping time, because when it was all said and done … no editing required.

○ **In disguise.** When creating a character on video that you'll talk to during the live lesson, it can be a fun extra if the person on video is actually you in disguise. Once we shot a professor character we called via "video-phone" during a K–1 lesson. In the video, Professor SmartyPants was played by the same teacher who spoke to the good doctor live during the lesson. We just added funny glasses, a moustache, a silly accent, and the latest in lab wear. While the kindergarteners wondered if it was really him, the more savvy first-graders giggled along, feeling like insiders on the gag.

THE MAN
OF 281
FACES

Method 18:

The Character Teach

Great creative characters have the quality of being especially memorable to kids. Mr. Noodle from recent episodes of *Sesame Street*. Robbie Rotten from *Lazytown*. And okay ... I'll admit it ... I still remember Morgan Freeman as "Vincent the Vegetable Vampire" in old episodes of *The Electric Company*.

Sometimes nobody can say it quite like a character.

It Works Like This

I still stand by what I said in chapter 10 ... characters typically work best in children's ministry when they're balanced with a "real" person, a teacher figure who's not pretending to be anybody. Once in a great while, however, a purely character-driven lesson can actually work rather nicely.

Maybe, instead of just teaching that construction-themed lesson as normal Mr. Mike, bring in a new teacher or teaching apprentice to teach it as "Tony, the Construction Worker."

For a mystery theme, "Sherlock Shoes," the detective, might make a nice teacher as kids uncover the clues surrounding the murder mystery of Cain and Abel.

Keep these three rules in mind, however, to make teaching characters come alive effectively.

1. No puppets teaching the whole lesson. Nada. Zilch. Ix-nay on the uppets-pay. Puppets make nice sidekicks, but the teaching needs to come out of the mouth of a human being.
2. Try to keep characters grounded in some sense of reality. A construction worker character rings true because he's still a real person. He just adds a little sawdust-flavored style to the lesson.

On the other hand, an alien teaching the lesson ... well, it's just too out there. It's hard for me to take Jesus-talk seriously when it's coming from a green-faced Martian.

3. No animals should teach the lesson. Animal characters in dramas or puppet plays may work well, but I don't want a wildebeest to lead the third-graders in their salvation prayer. Trust me, I've tried it. Can you spell *disaster*?

It Looks Like This

Example: Mission Unstoppable

This spy-themed unit taught by my pals Dave and Holly was the perfect character combo. They came out all decked-out as spies, using spy lingo, loaded up with spy gadgets, but at the end of the day, they were still Dave and Holly. They were still the teachers, but they were just having some spy fun. This is a great way to do character teaching, because it brings all the flavor of the character to the lesson, while still keeping the content rooted in reality.

Helpful Little Hint

○ *Character-izing your teaching script.* Don't feel like you have to chuck your entire teaching script and start over when you add a character. If your character "wouldn't say it like that," then make some simple adjustments to the script before the weekend rolls around. Rehearsal is a lifesaver for this because it gives you a chance to try a character on for size and work out the kinks. Maybe all the teaching script needs is a Brooklyn accent and a couple character catch-phrases added in to make it fit "Tony the Construction Worker" to a T.

Method 19:

Environments with Character

Envision a teaching space loaded to the rafters with character and possibility. You'll create an environment in which anything is possible—including transformational teaching!

It Works Like This

Think about *Pee-Wee's Playhouse*: talking chairs, maps, couches, and windows; bags and shelves loaded to the gills with all kinds of crazy props; a whole sideshow of zany characters who regularly drop in for a visit. Okay, maybe the genie is taking things a bit far, but still ... Even

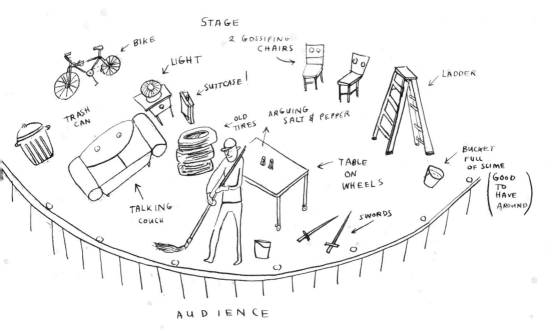

if you take Pee-Wee himself out of the mix and drop yourself into the setting in his place, you've got a recipe for fun teaching.

How about the *Blue's Clues* house? Talking salt and pepper shakers, side tables, and mailboxes. A letter-a-day (video letters, no less!) from friends. Clues to find. Paintings you can jump into. Who couldn't have fun teaching something in a setting like this?

Don't forget good old Mr. Rogers. As far as fun environments go, his pad had it goin' on. Who else has a trolley running through their living room, a Picture Picture that's really a video screen, and everybody in the neighborhood, from Mr. McFeely to Chef Brockett, dropping by for a visit. And we haven't even scratched the surface on The Land of Make-Believe.

These environments are all jam-packed with possibilities for creativity, characters, and fun. By dropping yourself smack-dab into the middle of similar circumstances, you'll be all set up for kid-friendly success.

It Looks Like This

Example: Scooter's Playhouse

A K–1 creation modeled after *Pee Wee's Playhouse*, this setting had it all … a talking dresser, toys and action figures for re-enacting Bible stories, a robot who spouted the prerecorded Bible verse in monotone robot-ese, and a word of the day (Pee-Wee Herman style … whenever the teacher says "giving," everybody screams). The teacher taught many Bible stories to his K–1 crowd from this fun-filled backdrop, and the creative possibilities were endless. To help illustrate the application, sometimes Professor SmartyPants would call on the videophone and talk about his trouble with the other professors. Props hung everywhere to assist with great Bible storytelling. The only thing missing was the kitchen sink … oh, wait … the playhouse had one of those too.

Example: Professor Wonder

What setting is more fun than a scientist's lab? Test tubes, beakers, and things that bubble and froth. The lab of Professor Wonder was another K–1 concoction, providing the perfect setting for kindergarten-friendly discussions on creation. And while Professor Wonder was an actual inhabitant of the lab (a character who helped teach), the main teacher remained a "real" person in the lab who helped draw the doc back to the Bible.

Helpful Little Hints

○ *Creating a monster.* It's so easy to get carried away, isn't it? Sometimes we start creating these fun-filled environments and we just get overexcited. We can't help it.

Be careful not to create a monster. While the potential for endless possibilities is what makes a character-driven environment such an appealing

DON'T CREATE ME!!!

place to teach, don't forget that a character-driven environment is an appealing place *to teach!* Let everything you do in your zany wonderland serve one purpose ... to clarify and strengthen the Bible teaching. Don't let the environment itself become the featured item on the menu. Remember, the Bible is the meaty main course, the creative setting is just the side dish. And maybe the dessert. And the mint afterward.

○ ***To be (me) or not to be (me).*** While you can certainly teach as a character from these madcap environments, don't overlook the power of just being yourself. It's easy to OD on characters and craziness. These fun-filled settings can have an awful lot going on, so, in the end, the strongest choice is often just to be you. By teaching as yourself, you'll root all the kookiness in reality and stop the fun from upstaging the Bible story.

Method 20:
Reader's Theater

Want to get dramatic, but seem to be tragically short on actors? Well, turn your frown upside down with this rehearsal-free way to stage a story.

It Works Like This

Set up some music stands along your stage, with a script on each one. Either use this method as a chance to break in some new teachers or teens, or call kids up out of the audience. Just be sure they can read well. Assign them parts and set them up behind the music stands.

Think of this as an old radio drama. The "actors" stand behind their music stands and dramatically read the lines. No blocking, no action. It works best when you have a little fun with them along the way, directing them, having them try out different ways of saying the lines, even adding silly sound effects into the mix.

It Looks Like This

Example: Cain and Abel

Here's a gander at a section of the Cain and Abel story, adapted for Reader's Theater. In this example, the teacher reads the Narrator part, but might also stop along the way to give unscripted direction or commentary to the actors.

BOOK
WORM

NARRATOR: TIME PASSED AND EVE GAVE BIRTH TO A SECOND SON. ADAM AND EVE WERE PLEASED. ONCE AGAIN, THEY WANTED TO CHOOSE A NAME THAT WOULD HONOR THEIR SON, WHOM THEY HOPED WOULD GROW UP TO MAKE THEM PROUD.

Lullaby music — quickly played

ADAM: I HAVEN'T BEEN "ABLE" TO COME UP WITH A NAME ...
EVE: ABEL! I LOVE IT! WHAT A WONDERFUL NAME.

SFX of sheep ... over the top, silly, maybe even a person doing sheep noises

ABEL: WHAT A FINE FLOCK OF SHEEP I HAVE.
NARRATOR: ... SAID ABEL ...
ABEL: OF COURSE, THERE ARE THOSE THAT ARE SMALLER THAN OTHERS AND THERE ARE THOSE THAT ARE MY MOST PRIZED AND VALUED. IF I WANT TO PLEASE GOD WITH AN OFFERING, I'D GIVE HIM A SHEEP WITH THE FATTEST PORTIONS.
NARRATOR: NOW, IN BIBLICAL TIMES, ANIMALS WERE OFTEN KILLED FOR GOD. IT WAS CONSIDERED A WAY TO WORSHIP GOD.

SFX of small hoe digging into a box of gravel

CAIN: I LABOR ALL DAY TO PRODUCE THE FEW CROPS THAT GROW HERE.
NARRATOR: ... SAID CAIN...
CAIN: I AM VERY BUSY ... AND NOW I MUST TAKE AN OFFERING TO GOD. I GUESS I WILL JUST HAVE TO HURRY AND THROW A BASKET OF FOOD TOGETHER SO I CAN BE DONE WITH IT! AHHGG, I DON'T HAVE TIME FOR THIS!

The audience-picked actors read the roles dramatically, even over-dramatically, adding distinct voices to each character. Granted … kids picked out of the audience aren't going to do this on their own, but as the teacher gives some silly direction along the ways, everyone's inner ham eventually floats to the surface.

Example: Nehemiah

Here's another variation on Reader's Theater, with the story of Nehemiah. You'll notice that this one is a little more heightened and a little more serious. This works great, but maybe not with kids right out of the audience. Something more stylized like this is better to try out on some up-and-coming teachers.

NARRATOR: OUR STORY BEGINS DURING A TIME OF BOTH GREAT HOPE AND GREAT DISTRESS FOR THE NATION OF ISRAEL. ISRAEL'S PEOPLE HAD BEEN IN EXILE FOR THE LAST 141 YEARS. THEY HAD BEEN TAKEN CAPTIVE BY VARIOUS LANDS AND SEPARATED FROM THEIR HOMELAND AND, IN MANY CASES, THEIR FAMILIES. ONE SUCH ISRAELITE WAS NEHEMIAH.

NEHEMIAH: YOUR WINE, MY LORD.

NARRATOR: NEHEMIAH WAS CUPBEARER TO ARTAXERXES, THE KING AND RULER OVER BABYLON AND THE ENTIRE PERSIAN EMPIRE. NEHEMIAH HAD BEEN BORN IN BABYLON. BUT AS NEHEMIAH GREW, HE WAS BLESSED WITH FAVOR BY GOD AND CAME INTO HIS PRESENT POSITION OF POWER AND RESPECT.

KING: NEHEMIAH.

NEHEMIAH: YES, MY KING.

KING: TELL ME MORE OF YOUR PEOPLE. OFTEN WE HAVE SPOKEN OF YOUR HOMELAND … ISRAEL, AND OF YOUR PEOPLE WHO HAVE RETURNED THERE. TELL ME OF THIS.

NEHEMIAH: WHAT YOU SPEAK OF IS VERY CLOSE TO MY HEART, MY LORD. AND YET, THERE IS LITTLE TO TELL.

KING: BUT I AM CURIOUS. GO ON.

NEHEMIAH: AS YOU KNOW, MY PEOPLE WERE TAKEN CAPTIVE BY BABYLON, DURING THE REIGN OF NEBUCHADNEZZAR. SINCE THEN WE HAVE BEEN SCATTERED THROUGHOUT THE PERSIAN EMPIRE, WHILE OUR HOMELAND SITS DESERTED AND FOREIGNERS MOVE IN.

KING: AHHH, YES.

NEHEMIAH: NINETY YEARS AGO OR SO, SOME TRIED TO RETURN TO JERUSALEM, BUT WITHOUT MUCH SUCCESS. PERHAPS THEY STAYED ... SEEKING OUT A LIVING.

KING: TRAGIC ... (TO HIMSELF) STRANGERS IN THEIR OWN LAND.

NEHEMIAH: YES.

KING: AND WHAT OF YOUR FAMILY?

NEHEMIAH: MY BROTHER HANANI LED ANOTHER GROUP BACK JUST 13 YEARS AGO, ALMOST TO THIS MONTH, BUT I KNOW NOTHING OF THEM. MY HOPE IS THAT THEY HAVE REBUILT THE CITY OF JERUSALEM TO ITS FORMER GLORY.

KING: BUT YOU DO NOT KNOW.

NEHEMIAH: NO. I CLING TO THE HOPE THAT ALL IS WELL, YET IT PAINS ME TO THINK THAT THE HOLY CITY OF JERUSALEM MAY SIT IN RUIN.

KING: I KNOW IT DOES, MY FRIEND.

For a great audio example of this style, listen to a prerecorded radio drama, like Focus on the Family's *The Lion, the Witch, and the Wardrobe*, which you can find on CD at *www.amazon.com*. It's a great model to follow.

Helpful Little Hints

HEE
HEE

HEE
HEE

○ *Laugh it up.* The trick is to not take yourself too seriously. You're not going to create high drama using Reader's Theater. Not without some rehearsal anyway. What you can create is a fun, even hilarious, way of telling the story using what you do have at your disposal: kids and a story. So cast yourself in the role of director for this makeshift pageant. Feel free to stop and give the kids a little silly direction along the way: "Say Nehemiah's line more like you just dropped your ice cream! . . . Yes, that's it! Continue!" That sort of thing.

HA
HA

HOO
HOO

HEE
HEE

HOO
HOO

○ *The highlight.* When calling on kids to participate in Reader's Theater, prep the scripts in advance by using a highlighter to make each character's lines stand out. Cain stands at one music stand, so make sure the script there has all of Cain's lines highlighted; same for all the other characters. This prevents kids from losing their place and trying to hunt down their lines. Also, tape character names to the front of each music stand. This helps kids in the audience follow along and remember who is who.

HA
HA

○ *Introductions, please!* Think about adding some silly intros at the beginning of each piece. Here's an example of this tomfoolery from the beginning of the Cain and Abel story:

ANNOUNCER: WELCOME TO GENESIS THEATER WHERE BIBLICAL STORIES COME TO LIFE. TONIGHT'S PROGRAM IS BROUGHT TO YOU BY TOMMY FIGLEAFER CLOTHING ... "WE'VE GOT YOU COVERED." TONIGHT'S CAST, IN ORDER OF APPEARANCE IS: _____ AS THE NARRATOR, _____ AS EVE, _____ AS ADAM AND CAIN, AND _____ AS GOD AND ABEL. LET'S JOIN TONIGHT'S PROGRAM WHICH IS ALREADY IN PROGRESS ...

◯ *Sound effect fun.* Sound effects are a great way to add both silliness and drama to this type of radio theater. For more schticky stories, have a sound-effects table set up with physical props … cowbells, coconut shells for horse hooves, a box of sand with a shovel … and assign someone to sound effects duty. You can also use standard CD or downloaded sound effects (see Sound Effects, page 243).

◯ *Fun with keyboards.* Some fancy-schmancy electronic keyboards come with built-in disk drives that store sound effects. You hit an A-flat and you get a duck quacking … that sort of thing. I've had wonderful success tracking down a keyboardist in the church who had one of these fabulous doodads. It puts a whole world of quick and easy sound effects right at your fingertips … literally.

A-OOOOGA !
A-OOOGA !

♪ ♪

WHACK!

HEE
HEE

HOO
HOO

HA
HA

Tweeeeet!

BLAM! CLUCK BOOP! TWING RING! ZING! HA HA HA HA HA HA HA BLIP! QUACK QUACK (SWEDISH DUCK) #∏木￥ (PEKING DUCK) 293

EPILOGUE

My heart **beats fast** to see kids transformed by the Bible.

My pulse **races** to see creative, experiential, relevant teaching hit kids right where it counts.

I am **left breathless** when I see teachers powering up, ready to pour their all into growing and strengthening their upfront skills so that kids will be left in awe by the Bible.

Never forget that you are part of a fabulous reinvention of Sunday school ... an unwavering and passionate commitment to creating transformational teaching.

Reinvent fearlessly. Leave kids doing life differently on Monday as a result of Sunday.

After all, that's what it comes down to, right?

A roomful of kids. All eyes focused in rapt attention on a teacher who delivers the Bible lesson with power, creativity, and authority. Kids blown away by God. Here and there a mouth hangs open as kids engage in the story of Boaz and Ruth with the kind of fervor usually reserved for their new Xbox 360. Kids who stride into Monday morning transformed by what they heard on Sunday. Kids who come into a relationship with God and have their eternal trajectories changed forever ...

There's only one word for a Sunday morning gig like that.

Fabulous.

APPENDIX

(that stuff at the back of the book)

The Handy Dandy
TRANSFORMATIONAL TEACHING
Evaluation Form

1. Getting on the Same Page

_____ (the teacher) and _____ (the evaluation buddy) agree that the purpose of this evaluation is ongoing development of teaching technique. The evaluation buddy commits to giving fearless and specific evaluation while cheering the teacher on to new heights of skill and technique.

2. Technique Focus

Pick one or two of these techniques to focus attention on for the next couple of months:

Techniques for Making Moments Happen

- ☐ Stepping into the story
- ☐ Contrast
- ☐ Intentional silence
- ☐ Handling the Bible
- ☐ Contemporizing the moment

Verbal Techniques

- ☐ Just talking
- ☐ Peaks and valleys
- ☐ Softening

Movement Techniques

- ☐ Defying drift
- ☐ Intentional movement
- ☐ Sitting for stress
- ☐ Positioning for strength
- ☐ Using levels

3. Today's Lesson

(Evaluation Buddy—Sit in on today's lesson. Watch the teacher with eyes open for the following three areas. Write down your observations. Be specific!)

List three specific moments or techniques where the teacher hit a home run.

1.

2.

3.

Jot down a couple changes that might strengthen the lesson for the next service (if you have one).

1.

2.

Now think development. Identify two or three specific moments where skill or technique may need to be developed and strengthened.

1.

2.

3.

4. Discuss Amongst Yourselves

After observing the lesson, sit down with the teacher to talk about what you saw. I'll give you a topic: Today's lesson ... ways it cooked and ways it could have cooked more.

Evaluation Form

1. Getting on the Same Page

_____*Joe*_____ (the teacher) and _____*Schmoe*_____ (the evaluation buddy) agree that the purpose of this evaluation is ongoing development of teaching technique. The evaluation buddy commits to giving fearless and specific evaluation while cheering the teacher on to new heights of skill and technique.

2. Technique Focus

Pick one or two of these techniques to focus attention on for the next couple of months:

Techniques for Making Moments Happen

- ☑ Stepping into the story
- ☐ Contrast
- ☐ Intentional silence
- ☐ Handling the Bible
- ☐ Contemporizing the moment

Verbal Techniques

- ☐ Just talking
- ☑ Peaks and valleys
- ☐ Softening

EXAMPLE

Movement Techniques

- ☐ Defying drift
- ☐ Intentional movement
- ☐ Sitting for stress
- ☐ Positioning for strength
- ☐ Using levels

3. Today's Lesson

(Evaluation Buddy—Sit in on today's lesson. Watch the teacher with eyes open for the following three areas. Write down your observations. Be specific!)

List three specific moments or techniques where the teacher hit a home run.

1. *That moment when you asked kids for their responses ... you had total control of the room. Two months ago they would have eaten you alive!!! Rock on!*

2. *Wow! The power and confidence in your teaching now that your lesson is memorized is uncanny. You can feel it in the kids' attention. They are glued to you.*

3. *No more drift. When you anchored yourself at the end of the story and delivered the application example about picking on a kid during the kickball game ... I actually got chills.*

Jot down a couple changes that might strengthen the lesson for the next service (if you have one).

1. *Check your wording on the Bible verse. You stumbled when you said it. You may also want to put it on the screen behind you for visual reinforcement.*

2. *I think you forgot to pray at the end.*

Now think development. Identify two or three specific moments where skill or technique may need to be developed and strengthened.

1. *Let's work together on higher peaks in your story. There were moments of excitement that you didn't treat any differently than the rest in terms of energy, pacing, excitement. I think we're missing a couple powerful moments! It's growing though. It really is!*

2. *When you get to the part of the story where the guards are mocking Jesus ... BECOME the guards. You're staying outside the moment, and that's distancing us from the potency here. Remember to step into the story and tell it from the inside.*

4. Discuss Amongst Yourselves

After observing the lesson, sit down with the teacher to talk about what you saw. I'll give you a topic: Today's lesson ... ways it cooked and ways it could have cooked more.

PERSONAL DEVELOPMENT PLAN FOR TEACHERS

(where am i going and what does it all mean?)

As you tackle the techniques in this book, this personal development plan can serve as a road map. While I hope the potential in these techniques excites and encourages you toward dynamic growth, it's critical not to get overwhelmed along the way. Don't try to incorporate more than two or three new techniques at once.

Here are some steps to follow as you figure out where to start:

TAKE A CLOSE-UP LOOK

First things first. Get a clear idea on what techniques you do well, and where you want to grow. Watch yourself on video. Spend a couple weeks with your evaluation buddy getting your bearings. Talk about what's working and where you want to focus your attention.

- 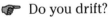 Do you drift?
- What natural speech pattern rhythms may be keeping you from creating exciting peaks and valleys?
- What prevents you from achieving powerful moments in your teaching? Do you tend to narrate stories from the outside versus stepping into the stories? Could you use silence for impact? How about contrast?

MAKE MEMORIZATION A PRIORITY

This is one of the single biggest factors in developing your teaching skills. As long as you're focused on the words, the upfront techniques will always take second place. But master memorization, and you see exponential growth ... guaranteed.

SET SOME GOALS

Pick one or two main techniques on which to focus your attention on over the next two or three months. Focus your attention heavily on these techniques. In partnership with your evaluation buddy (see pages 300—301), go to battle on these two or three of these. Here are some great places to start:

☞ If you struggle with drift, focus on anchoring yourself more for the next two months.

☞ Work on breaking out of your natural speech rhythm to create big peaks and valleys. Push yourself out of your comfort zone into more extreme moments.

☞ Pick one technique for making moments happen. Maybe work on stepping into the story more.

Developing skills takes time, so don't get discouraged. Remember, you're breaking old habits. Have your evaluation buddy hold you accountable for growth in these areas. And when you see progress and growth? High fives all around. Okay, splurge ... high tens. You deserve it.

LAYER ON NEW TECHNIQUES

After two or three months, you'll see real changes. Old habits start to die. New instincts replace them. You feel a difference in the kids' attention, as you bring the Bible to life in ever more effective ways.

Now it's time to pick one or two new techniques to layer into the mix. Some possibilities:

☞ If you've conquered drift, work on making your movement especially intentional. Incorporate more levels and places to sit for stress.

☞ Play with contrast and silence. Find powerful moments to bring these techniques to life.

After six months of intentional development, debrief your progress with your evaluation buddy or ministry leader. Watch a video of yourself from six months earlier and a video of last week's lesson. Celebrate the difference! Share the learnings with your team and your leader. Show them the videos! Strut your stuff . . . you are teaching with transformational power!

SPICE THINGS UP WITH VARIETY

Continually put the 20 different ways to teach the Bible creatively (chapter 12) to the test. Each of these creative methods can push and stretch you in unique ways. Each offers a new canvas to explore as you develop your art. You have a masterpiece to paint. No one can paint it as well as you.

A TRAINING GUIDE FOR MINISTRY LEADERS

(putting the techniques to the test)

This section isn't filled with warm fuzzy question to discuss or deep spiritual analogies.

Not many anyway.

The best way I know how to train and develop teachers for dynamic teaching is to get up and do it. Try techniques on for size, work them out through practice, critique, and analysis. Seeing is believing. Doing is growing.

Consider offering a two-hour teacher-development workshop once a month or even once every two weeks. Ask teachers to read a chapter of this book prior to the workshop. In some cases you may decide to tackle two chapters in a single session … it's up to you. Then engage your teaching team in training and development. Here are some chapter-by-chapter ideas of how to maximize the impact of your workshop time.

CHAPTER 1: COMMITTED TO MEMORY

1. Do some serious self scrutiny before this training session. Ask yourself:

   - Do I believe that the practice of memorization would increase the level of excellence in our ministry?
   - If I do, what's keeping me from making this a shared value and expectation for every teacher? Am I afraid? Do I think people

will quit? What's the worst that could happen? What's the best that could happen?

2. Ask two teachers to come to this training session prepared to deliver a memorized lesson. Not a full one. A baby one. Maybe ten minutes' worth.

3. Briefly discuss the chapter with your teaching team. Ask:

   ■ What do you think about the benefits of memorization?
   ■ How many of you disagree with the concept of memorization? Why? (It's okay, you can say it. I know some of you hate the whole idea. Share. Open up. Purge.)
   ■ Do you believe that memorization would really lead to excellence?
   ■ Do you think the payoff could really be worth it? Why? Why not?

4. Use a little surprise to demonstrate the impact of memorization.

   ■ Have the script or notes from a sample lesson handy (a different lesson for each of the teachers, but not the lesson your two teachers have memorized). Spring this lesson on your two teachers, and have them deliver the lesson, using the script or notes.
   ■ Now have the teachers present the lessons they memorized.

5. Discuss the difference. Let the two teachers share their thoughts first.

   ■ What was the difference in the preparation process?
   ■ What was the difference in the moments of teaching?
   ■ Then let the rest of the teachers share their observations.
   ■ What were the differences as a spectator?
   ■ Which lesson would have the most potential of impacting kids—the memorized lesson or the non-memorized one?

6. Cast a clear vision with your team about where *you* stand on the

issue of memorization. If you believe memorization will take your ministry to new heights, you must lead your teachers there.

CHAPTER 2: THE PRACTICE OF PRACTICING

1. Even if the practice of rehearsal isn't currently an every week thing in your ministry, you've probably experienced it once or twice—the Christmas musical, the Easter pageant. Discuss as a team what you learned from those rehearsals.

   ▪ What were the wins?
   ▪ What were the losses?

2. Give each teacher a sheet of flip-chart paper and send them alone to separate parts of the room. Their assignment: Design an ongoing rehearsal schedule for your ministry. Ask them to incorporate midweek rehearsal, weekend rehearsal, and a run-through. You do this too. Give everyone 15 minutes.

3. Tape the sheets on the wall side by side. Have each person give a two-minute explanation and description of their model.

4. After everyone has shared, you may discover that many of the sample rehearsal schedules share similarities. Discuss the similarities.

5. On a blank sheet, draw out a new model that incorporates all the similarities.

6. Decide as a team:

   ▪ What wins might we experience if we incorporate a weekly rehearsal schedule like this one? List them out.
   ▪ What losses might we experience? List them out.

7. Now, here's a value-driven question. After discussing and processing the practice of rehearsal, do you value the idea for your ministry? Commit to making an intentional decision about what your ministry's stand will be on holding rehearsals.

CHAPTER 3: THE ART OF EVALUATION

1. Find one teacher who is willing to engage in an evaluation process in front of the team during this session. Ask the teacher to prepare and memorize a lesson.

2. Find another teacher who will give you permission to videotape his or her lesson. Put a camcorder in the back of the room and tape the lesson a couple weeks before this session.

3. During this session, invite the team to talk about any fears they may have of evaluation.

   - Does the idea of evaluation freak you out?
   - If it does, what specifically is intimidating about this process?
   - Does the idea of developing your skills appeal to you? Why or why not?

4. Model evaluation. Have the volunteer teacher present his or her lesson to the group, as if teaching kids on the weekend. Using the evaluation form (pages 298–299) as a guide, conduct a ten-minute evaluation right there in front of everyone. Remember:

   - Start with the good stuff. As the evaluation buddy, you are the teacher's biggest fan!
   - Focus then on changes that might be needed for a next service, if you have one.
   - Finally, jump into development. Ask the teacher to try that moment again, incorporating silence or intentional movement or another technique. Development is the key!

5. Acknowledge that the evaluation isn't perfect. This kind of vulnerable trust takes time. Ask the teacher who was evaluated to share his or her experience. Was it scary? Was it exciting?

6. Watch the video of the other teacher. Remind everyone of the rules of evaluation and practice a group evaluation afterward. Give the team permission to comment and give feedback. Be mindful of

letting things spiral into a nit-picky critique free-for-all. Remember, the goal is uplifting development.

7. Finally, talk about a possible evaluation arrangement specific to your teachers. What would work best?

   ▪ Partnering up with an evaluation buddy? Who would that be for each person?
   ▪ Group evaluation via video?
   ▪ Comparative evaluation? Has anyone seen videos of dynamic creative teaching that we should all look at together?

CHAPTER 4: REINVENTING YOUR ROTATION STRATEGY

So much of the success of the first three practices depends on freeing up time for your teachers. A strategic rotation structure can do just that.

1. Have three different white boards or flip charts in this session.

   ▪ On the first, draw your current teaching rotation on the whiteboard. Use the illustrations on page 54 as a guide.
   ▪ On the second, draw out The Whole-Weekend Approach, putting specific teacher names and times in the diagram. Again, refer to the rotation strategy illustrations from the chapter as an example.
   ▪ Just for fun, draw The Whole-Unit Approach as it could conceivably play out on your team.

2. Talk about what you see. Read through the pros and cons from chapter 4 for each scenario. Would they apply to your ministry? Why or why not?

3. Move toward a clear decision about which rotation structure would be the most ideal for your team. Which model would lead to an atmosphere of excellence? Set a deadline by which you will initiate this new rotation strategy.

4. Revisit the issues of memorization and rehearsal. What ramifications does a new rotation strategy have for freeing up memorization and rehearsal time for teachers?

CHAPTER 5: PLANNING POWERFUL PROGRAMS

1. Videotape two different weekend lessons prior to meeting. Bring the tapes to this training session and watch the lessons as a team.

   ■ Does the lesson incorporate all three learning styles?
   ■ Is the rule of using three different creative approaches at work here?
   ■ Is the application clear, specific, and practical to a kid's life?
   ■ Would a style makeover give the lesson new life or freshness?

2. Pull out the curriculum for an upcoming lesson. Read it together. Spend 30 minutes working it over, figuring out ways it could be adapted and planned based on the what you learned in chapter 5.

3. What would it look like for your team to meet together regularly for the purpose of powerful planning? Throw a couple different possible scenarios on paper. Would such a meeting involve the whole team? Just the teachers? Each individual teacher with the leader? Talk out the possibilities.

CHAPTER 6: MAKING MOMENTS! HAPPEN

1. Have two teachers each prepare and memorize a different lesson to deliver in this session. Make sure they are storytelling lessons like the story of David and Goliath from chapter 6, as opposed to concept-driven lessons. Have the teachers present the lesson to the group, doing it as if kids were in the room. Feel free to use the lessons from the "Technique in Action" section of the chapter.

2. "Workshop" the lessons. In other words, pick one or two techniques from chapter 6 and work on strengthening them in the lesson. Go

back to specific moments in the lesson and ask the teachers to do them again, putting the techniques more powerfully into play. Spend about 25 minutes on each teacher.

3. Be careful not to overwhelm the teachers. Focus on only one or two techniques or moments, but then work them over and over again, drawing out the power of the moments. Use the "Technique in Action" sections of chapter 5 as a model.

CHAPTER 7: TIPS FOR THE TONGUE

1. Same approach as used for chapter 6, but with two new teachers. The goal for your sessions on chapters 6, 7, and 8 is to work out techniques by doing them. Ask two new teachers each prepare and memorize a different lesson to deliver in this session. Have the teachers present the lesson to the group, as if kids were in the room. Feel free to use the lessons modeled in the "Technique in Action" section of the chapter.

2. "Workshop" the lessons, learning from your experiences in the chapter 7 session. Pick one or two techniques from chapter 7 and work on strengthening them in the lesson. Especially work on peaks and valleys. Most teachers tend to live vocally in their comfort zone, so push them to high highs and low lows. Spend about 25 minutes on each teacher.

3. Remember, don't overwhelm. Focus on only one or two techniques or moments for each but then work them over and over again, drawing out the power of the moments.

CHAPTER 8: MASTERING MOVEMENT

1. Ask every teacher to prepare and memorize a partial lesson, no more than two paragraphs. Allow about ten minutes to work on each teacher's lesson excerpt.

2. Focus on movement by applying the principles from the chapter.

- Challenge teachers who drift to anchor. Ask them to do the lesson again and again, breaking drifty habits and pushing themselves toward power.
- Challenge teachers who don't move at all to choose intentional movement. Push each teachers toward movement-oriented peaks and valleys.
- Look for places to sit for stress.
- Play with level ideas.

3. Talk about the experience of actually practicing these techniques over the last three sessions.

- How has practicing these techniques impacted your weekend lessons?
- How do you feel about the experience of working out the techniques in front of each other? Is it exciting? Scary? Do you feel more confident now than you did the first time you did it?

CHAPTER 9: RELEVANCE: KEEPING CURRENT

Before this session, give some homework. Assign each teacher to do a different relevance practice discussed in the chapter. Have one pick up *Disney Magazine* and read it from cover to cover. Have another spend a school-day afternoon hanging out at McDonalds and listening to kids speak. Have another rent video games and play them with his or her kids.

- What did you read, see, hear, or experience during your exploration of relevance?
- What new learning did you walk away with by immersing yourself in a kid's world?

Chances are good that this chapter pushed buttons and challenged some thinking among your teachers. Talk about that.

- What ideas in the chapter were new?
- Are there any ideas with which you disagree?
- What ideas seem easy to incorporate?
- Name one or two specific insights (things you heard kids say at McDonald's, aha moments while playing the PS2 with your son, etc.) that will change the way you relate to and teach kids on Sunday.

CHAPTER 10: CHANGING DIAPERS? CHANGING LIVES! PRESCHOOL PRINCIPLES

While it's easy to embrace new thoughts that don't require much change or reinvention, we sometimes file other ideas in the "not for us" side of our brains, just because we've never done them or they may require more integrated changes to the way we do ministry. Here's an exercise to bubble up some of those assumptions on your preschool team.

1. Give each teacher a differently colored packet of Post-It notes. Give them ten minutes to silently and individually write down their five biggest ahas from chapter 10 (one aha per Post-It note).

2. Have two flip charts. Write "Perfect Idea for Us" across the top of one, and "Great Idea, but Not for Us" across the top of the other.

3. Ask the team to share and explain their ahas. Have them post them on the appropriate board, based on whether the new thinking is something that they think would and should be incorporated into your ministry. Put the ideas that might not work for you or may not seem just right for your ministry on the "Not for Us" board.

4. Talk about why the "Not for Us" stuff landed on that board. Challenge the thinking. Did some things land there just because they've never been tried before? Should they be? Consider moving some Post-Its to the "Perfect Idea for Us" board.

5. Some of these ideas may be easy adjustments, but others might be more involved changes that require a little reworking or reinvention. So get practical. What steps could be taken in the next two months to incorporate some of the new ideas into the preschool ministry? Discuss what could and should be done and put a deadline to it.

CHAPTER 11: TECH TECHNIQUES

1. Discuss together the concept of decor.

- What areas of our ministry could be enhanced by some of the decor principles that chapter 11 explores? Where could texture be applied? How could signage be changed? Don't limit your discussion to teaching rooms. Think about hallways and main thoroughfares of the ministry as well.
- What perceptions might parents and kids have of our ministry based only on our decor choices. Does our decor scream excellence? Why or why not?
- How do we feel about spending time and money on frequently changing teaching props and sets? What would it look like to create one exciting but generic, all-purpose teaching space?

2. Discuss with your teachers the role that tech currently plays in teaching.

- Do we currently use tech? On a scale of 1 to 10, with 1 being finger puppets and flashlights, and 10 being a Broadway show, where are we on the continuum? Where do we want to be?
- Where could we make some easy tech upgrades? Or are tech upgrades unnecessary at this stage?
- What tech toys would be worth building into next year's budget? How can we plan ahead to move our ministry gradually forward in the area of tech?

CHAPTER 12: TWENTY WAYS TO TEACH THE BIBLE CREATIVELY

Give five of your teachers a single lesson prior to this session. Exact same lesson, exact same story, exact same teaching script. For time's sake, maybe only include the story and the application ... a partial lesson. Assign each of them to prepare it using a different creative method. Have one do Audience Participation. Have another do a One-Man Show. Game Show. Art Attack. Visual Props.

When you gather for this session, have a creativity marathon: have each teacher present their lesson to the others, as if kids were in the room. Take up to an hour and a half for this.

Even though the scripts were identical, the stories the same, you'll be amazed at how unique and varied each lesson was. Pick apart the nuances. Brainstorm other lessons in your curriculum that each method could readily be applied to.

Remind your team of this powerful principle: a single creative teacher is the foundation of any lesson. If you don't have a drama team, a worship team, tech bells and whistles ... if there's nothing else except a single gifted teacher and a roomful of kids, then you can have dynamic powerful creative teaching. Chapter 12 is built on that principle. There's no mention of actors or worship teams or puppetry. These elements are *wonderful* things ... but they only support the main event.

Dynamic creative transformational teaching.

RESOURCES

(where to find cool stuff)

AARON REYNOLDS TRAINING AND MINISTRY CONSULTING

I've had the privilege of traveling into local churches all around the world, helping to equip children's ministries to do dynamic life-changing teaching. So if you like what you've read, and you want to talk about me coming into your ministry to do some training workshops or to consult with your ministry, give me a holler. I'd love to talk. You can reach me through the "Aaron Reynolds" website:

www.creativekidsministry.com.

VIDEO TEACHING FOR COMPARATIVE EVALUATION

These DVDs are great to look at for comparing teaching skills and getting a grasp on the delivery techniques discussed in chapter 2. As you watch, keep in mind that these were shot for video, and therefore incorporate some things you can't replicate in live teaching. So focus on the teaching techniques ... look for peaks and valleys, how the teachers use movement, how they tell a personal story, how they use pacing and energy. Those are the techniques worth looking at closely.

- **FLIPT.** This ten-week DVD curriculum features great dynamic teaching by the Promiseland Team from Willow Creek Church. Available at *www.promiselandonline.com.*
- **NOOMA.** A series of DVDs featuring the teaching of pastor and

author Rob Bell. While these videos are targeted to adults, there's no denying the teaching techniques at work here can be applied to teaching any age. Available at Christian bookstores and online from *www.nooma.com* and *www.willowcreek.com*.

- **Rescue 911 and Rock Solid.** These video curriculums feature Craig Jutila, pastor of children's ministry at Saddleback Church, teaching in a variety of locations. It offers some nice models of good teaching in action. Available at *www.empoweringkids.net*.

SOUND EFFECTS

Sound Effect CDs

- **Killer Tracks** (*www.killertracks.com*). Incredible SFX that can be purchased by the set or individually. Awesome quality.
- **Hanna-Barbera Cartoon Sound Effects** by Hanna-Barbera. CD with 100 great cartoony SFX. Great for game shows. Available at *www.amazon.com*.
- **Hilarious Comical Effect, Vol. 1.** Audio CD with 101 fun sounds, also great for game shows. Available at *www.amazon.com*.

Downloadable Sound Effects

- **Sound Dogs** (*www.sounddogs.com*). Top notch SFX. You can preview the sounds right on the site before buying. Easy to search and reasonably priced. They also carry production music and CDs.
- **Sound Rangers** (*www.soundrangers.com*). Great SFX you can hear right on the site for about $1.45 apiece. A great site to return to again and again.

MUSIC

Soundtrack CDs

- **Chicago Bulls Greatest Hits.** Audio CD with 26 high energy tracks, perfect for walk-in music, game shows, and high-energy transitions between teaching elements. Available at *www.amazon.com.*

- **Jock Jams, Vol. 1 and 2.** Crowd pumpin' high-energy audio CD. A staple CD for great kid-friendly, crowd-rockin' fun. Available at *www.amazon.com.*

- **Stadium Anthems: Music for the Fans.** Some of the songs on this CD are dogs, but there's still enough great kid-friendly jams on here to make it worthwhile. Stuff like "Who Let the Dogs Out" by the Baha Men, "Start the Commotion" by the Wiseguys, and "The Power" by Snap make this worth having at the ready. Available at *www.amazon.com.*

- *Henry V.* Original soundtrack to the Kenneth Branagh movie of Shakespeare's classic. Shakespeare, you say? Don't be fooled. This CD is packed with dynamic dramatic music for more moody storytelling. Jesus in the garden? Good Friday? Moses and the plagues? It's like it was written for it. Available at *www.amazon.com.*

- *The Prince of Egypt.* Powerful, all-purpose dramatic storytelling music. I especially like track eight.

- *Batman.* A little funkier, but still makes great storytelling music.

- **Disney's *Tarzan* Soundtrack.** Some great percussive tracks on this one. Of course, there are the songs with voices, but skip past those and listen to the instrumental stuff.

- **Blue Man Group.** At last count, there were two or three CDs out by this blue-faced theater group. Very cool stuff.

Downloadable Production Music

- **Sound Rangers** (*www.soundrangers.com*). Nice production music for game shows and storytelling background scores. Very user-friendly site … just listen, buy, and download. Reasonably priced music too.

Sources for Great Production Music CD Sets

☞ **Killer Tracks** (*www.killertracks.com*). Unbelievably high quality SFX and production music. Really cool stuff. You can order a free demo from the website with samples and details on ordering.

TECH TOYS

Stage Lighting

☞ **Stage Lighting Store** (*www.stagelightingstore.com*). Great beginners' source for theater lighting options.

☞ **Cheap DJ Lights** (*www.cheapdjlights*). Another inexpensive source for starter stage lighting.

☞ **EPartyunlimited.com** (*www.epartyunlimited.com/visual-effects. html*). Lighting toys like strobes, fire pots, and spinning color wheels.

☞ **123dj** (*www.123dj.com*). Advanced lighting options, including intelligent programmable lights and tons of toys.

☞ Don't forget to check **eBay** for good steals on tech supplies.

Sound Samplers

☞ **Tweakalizer DFX69** (*www.123dj.com/roland/dfx69.html*). A really cool and affordable SFX sampler.

☞ **Boss SP303 Dr. Sample** (*www.guitar.com.au/effects/boss/ sp303_b.htm*).

☞ **Boss SP505** (*www.guitar.com.au/effects/boss/SP–505.htm*).

DJ Mixers

☞ *www.zzounds.com/cat—DJ-Mixers—2458*

Willow Creek Association

Vision, Training, Resources for Prevailing Churches

This resource was created to serve you and to help you build a local church that prevails. It is just one of many ministry tools that are part of the Willow Creek Resources® line, published by the Willow Creek Association together with Zondervan.

The Willow Creek Association (WCA) was created in 1992 to serve a rapidly growing number of churches from across the denominational spectrum that are committed to helping unchurched people become fully devoted followers of Christ. Membership in the WCA now numbers over 12,000 Member Churches worldwide from more than ninety denominations.

The Willow Creek Association links like-minded Christian leaders with each other and with strategic vision, training, and resources in order to help them build prevailing churches designed to reach their redemptive potential. Here are some of the ways the WCA does that.

- **A2: Building Prevailing Acts 2 Churches—Today**—an annual two-and-a-half day event, held at Willow Creek Community Church in South Barrington, Illinois, to explore strategies for building churches that reach out to seekers and build believers, and to discover new innovations and breakthroughs from Acts 2 churches around the country.

- **The Leadership Summit**—a once a year, two-and-a-half-day conference to envision and equip Christians with leadership gifts and responsibilities. Presented live at Willow Creek as well as via satellite broadcast to over one hundred locations across North America, this event is designed to increase the leadership effectiveness of pastors, ministry staff, volunteer church leaders, and Christians in the marketplace.

- **Ministry-Specific Conferences**—throughout each year the WCA hosts a variety of conferences and training events—both at Willow Creek's main campus and offsite, across the U.S., and around the world—targeting church leaders and volunteers in ministry-specific areas such as: evangelism, small groups, preaching and teaching, the arts, children, students, women, volunteers, stewardship, raising up resources, etc.

- **Willow Creek Resources®**—provides churches with trusted and field-tested ministry resources in such areas as leadership, evangelism, spiritual formation, spiritual gifts, small groups, stewardship, student ministry, children's ministry, the use of the arts-drama, media, contemporary music—and more.

- **WCA Member Benefits**—includes substantial discounts to WCA training events, a 20 percent discount on all Willow Creek Resources®, *Defining Moments* monthly audio journal for leaders, quarterly *Willow* magazine, access to a Members-Only section on WillowNet, monthly communications, and more. Member Churches also receive special discounts and premier services through WCA's growing number of ministry partners—Select Service Providers—and save an average of $500 annually depending on the level of engagement.

For specific information about WCA conferences, resources, membership, and other ministry services contact:

Willow Creek Association
P.O. Box 3188, Barrington, IL 60011-3188
Phone: 847-570-9812, Fax: 847-765-5046
www.willowcreek.com